Matilda Harrison

The Poet's Wreath

Selections of Poems

Matilda Harrison

The Poet's Wreath
Selections of Poems

ISBN/EAN: 9783337006563

Printed in Europe, USA, Canada, Australia, Japan

Cover: Foto ©Thomas Meinert / pixelio.de

More available books at **www.hansebooks.com**

THE POET'S WREATH,

BEING

A SELECTION OF POEMS.

BY

Matilda Harrison.

[Copyright.]

The Poet's soul on wings of light
Can soar beyond these shades of night.

BLACKBURN:
"EXPRESS AND STANDARD" GENERAL PRINTING WORKS.
1890.

DEDICATED

TO THE MEMORY OF THE LATE

Benjamin Hargreaves, Esq.,

OF ARDEN HALL, ACCRINGTON.

AROUND THE REVER'D MEMORY OF THAT GOOD MAN
I TWINE MY HUMBLE WREATH OF POESY,
IN FOND REMEMBRANCE OF HIS BEAUTIFUL AND CONSISTENT LIFE,
AND IN
HONOURABLE ACKNOWLEDGMENT OF THOSE RARE CHRISTIAN VIRTUES,
THE DAILY PRACTICE OF WHICH
THREW AROUND THAT LIFE A SINGULARLY SWEET AND MYSTICAL CHARM,
AND WON FOR HIM THE RESPECT AND ADMIRATION
OF ALL WHO CAME WITHIN
THE RADIANT SPHERE OF HIS TRULY CHRISTIAN NATURE.
MY EARLY RECOLLECTIONS OF A TRULY GOOD MAN
ARE CONNECTED WITH HIM;
AND MUCH OF THE INSPIRATION OF MY EARLIEST POEMS
I CAN TRACE TO THE CONTEMPLATION OF HIS GRAND AND NOBLE
CHARACTER, WHICH HAS WREATH'D HIS NAME
WITH A HALO OF UNDYING SPLENDOUR AND BEAUTY,
WHICH NOT ONLY ON EARTH BUT IN THE ARCHIVES OF HEAVEN
SHINES WITH EVER ENHANCING RADIANCE,
TO THE HONOUR AND GLORY OF HIS GOD FOR EVER.

MATILDA HARRISON.

In Memoriam—Benjamin Hargreaves.

"They rest from their labours."

Repose, noble soul ! thou art worthy of rest ;
Thy much-honour'd name shall the working man bless ;
Thy deeds of benevolence, mercy, and love
Shall add to thy joy in the kingdom above.

The last of a noble house, bounteous and free,
The virtues of one and all centred in thee ;
Thy well-spent existence that lov'd name has wreath'd
In a halo most sacred by grateful hearts breath'd.

If prayers were still needed thy bliss to augment,
Many lives thou hast cheer'd in that work would be spent ;
Many hearts thou hast gladden'd, and homes thou hast blest,
Will blend thy dear name in their visions of rest.

Ease tempted thee not—it might well have been thine ;
Wealth held not for thee the charms most divine ;
Thy unselfish life to His honour was spent,
Who in infinite goodness thy talents had lent.

And well hast thou render'd thy Maker His due,
In a life of strict rectitude, faithful and true :
In a glorious endeavour life's ills to assuage,
Thy name stands recorded on heaven's vast page.

Poor hungry ones often thy bounteous hand fed ;
The sinful and erring thy counsel oft led ;
The fatherless found thee a friend in their need—
The widow rejoiced in a patron indeed.

No trumpet voice sounded thy praises around ;
On the flag of ambition thy name was not found ;
In silence and secret thy goodness was shown,
Sufficient for thee that to God it was known.

And now with life's journey most valiantly run,
The work He had given thee most faithfully done,
Well pleased is thy Saviour such service to own,
And rewards thee at last with a kingdom and crown.

PREFACE.

AT the earnest entreaty and through the kind assistance of many friends, I submit this, my first book, to the critical eye of the public; and in doing so I beg the kind indulgence of those who have happily had the advantages of education, for I have not; and I only state the fact here because I think the knowledge of it will help them to excuse any error of composition which their superior training may enable them to detect.

In answer to the oft repeated question as to how I write these Poems, I may honestly say I cannot tell; I only know that at certain times, and under certain influences, there is the unfolding of a higher nature—the rolling away of the mists and shadows of earth, and the conscious and exquisite delight of a more congenial existence in the higher and sublimer realms of thought—then, and then only, can I write. There is then no difficulty; nay, the difficulty would be in suppressing the natural desire and tendency to speak my thoughts in poetry.

MATILDA HARRISON.

THE POET'S WREATH.

THE ANGEL'S WREATH.

I sat me in twilight's poetical hour,
To await the poetical tide :
But a mass of confusion pervaded my mind,
And a subject I could not decide.
Impatient, I laid down the pen to withdraw
From a task that so fruitless would seem,
When a voice whispered near me, "Stay, mortal, oh, stay ;
I'll weave thee a beautiful dream."

With the words came a feeling of exquisite bliss,
And the mortal sight closed to the world :
But, instead of confusion or chaos, indeed,
A most wonderful vision unfurled.
Before me, transcendantly radiant, there stood
A being of holier mould,
Entwining a wreath of magnificence rare,
Of grandeur and beauty untold.

Each floweret sent forth a most brilliant ray,
Never borrow'd from rainbow or sun ;
Each petal outshone the earth's costliest gems,
Or a thousand such merged into one.
Each leaf seem'd a mirror of radiant light,
Revealing fresh wonders to view ;
Whilst traced 'mid its delicate blossoms so fair
Shone the words, " Ever faithful and true."

I asked the bright being for whose honour'd head
He had twined such a coronet rare.
He smiled as he answer'd, for one who is not
To the world either wealthy or fair ;
But one who has wept 'neath its cold bitter scorn,
And borne her full share of its sorrow ;
But ever remember'd earth's dreariest night
Would be lost in a glorious morrow.

For one who has wrought out a beautiful life
By a thousand and one noble deeds,
Whose name never shone in the records which boast
Of empty profession or creeds.
Enshrined in the hearts of earth's suffering ones,
Entwin'd in the sinner's last prayer,
Inscribed in celestial annals of fame
Is the name that my garland must bear.

I have watch'd through the years of her mortal career
With a joy ye on earth cannot know,
And the light of her faith has shone clearest and best
'Mid the darkness of earth's bitter woe.
Unselfish and true, with a heart that can feel
For a weak, erring sister or brother,
Whose highest ambition is only to spend
And be spent for the good of another.

Though humble her birth, she has liv'd to adorn
The ranks of the poor and the lowly,
And honour'd the name of our Father and God
By a life most devoted and holy.
The world knows her not, for she joins not the throng
Who worship ambition and fame,
But trac'd by immortal hands, fadeless and bright,
Shines for ever that poor toiler's name.

These beautiful flowerets are truly her own,
And spring from her beautiful life,
They are sown in the thousand and one loving acts
That lighten the earth's bitter strife.
Dream not that your lives are a secret untold,
For sure as the sun follows rain,
So sure shall ye reap what on earth ye have sown,
Be the fruit either pleasure or pain.

Mark well the rich gems of my garland so fair,
Watch carefully through the bright range,
And know that some scene of a life is reveal'd
In each varied and wonderful change ;
'Tis thus we can judge of your spiritual life,
No matter your form or your creed,
The laws that obtain in these realms of the soul
Are unerring and faithful indeed.

But my crown is complete, and awaits but the time
When its beautiful wearer shall cease
From trials so nobly endur'd on the earth
And enter her haven of peace ;
Rouse now to thy work, bid the earth-toilers learn
To weave out life's purposes well,
And the wherefore of much that so puzzles them now,
The unveiling of spirits shall tell.

With a smile that still lingers he wav'd an adieu,
And away to some happier sphere,
And the sad dreary hum of this discordant world
Broke mournfully over my ear ;
Yet oft as fond memory brings back the scene
Of that Angel-wreath'd coronet rare,
I ask if in all the wide world there can be
One fitted those jewels to wear.

A WASTED LIFE.

Nay, ask me not to leave this grave,
    Kind sexton, let me stay ;
'Tis all of earth I ask or crave,
    Beside this mound to pray.

I've wander'd many a dreary mile,
    To reach this hallow'd spot ;
To rest my weary soul awhile,
    Kind sir, forbid it not.

Here lie the dreams of happier years,
    Here richest treasures sleep ;
Oh, could I win them back with tears,
    I would for ever weep.

I was not always what I seem,
    A poor besotted slave ;
Life once was like a poet's dream,
    With scarce one ruffled wave.

A father's joy, a mother's pride,
    I passed my earliest years,
With scarce one childish wish denied,
    Or cause for childish tears.

But in the giddy whirl of youth,
    'Neath fortune's golden spell,
I turn'd aside from paths of truth,
    I gambled, drank, and fell.

I broke my gentle mother's heart,
    I bow'd my father's head ;
I play'd a cruel, treacherous part,
    Would God I'd died instead.

Once more an angel to my side,
    In tenderest pity came ;
Man never won a lovelier bride,
    Or wreck'd one fairer name.

This church records my marriage vow,
    Those bells rang out my bliss ;
Great God, that mortal man should bow,
    And sink so low as this.

That stately hall across the way
    Was once my father's pride ;
'Twas there he spent his lifelong day,
    'Twas there he droop'd and died.

There, too, I made my wife her home,
    And vow'd no earthly power
Should tempt me from her side to roam,
    Or cause one sorrow's hour.

A few brief years I answer'd well
    No home could happier be,
No tongue my Ada's love could tell,
    None knew how dear to me.

Oh, Memory, cease thy backward roll,
    Mar not those years so fair ;
In mercy to my tortur'd soul,
    Thy last dread torture spare.

But no, the faithful tide rolls on,
    Earth's fairest scenes are past,
The last fond smile of love is gone,
    I stand alone at last.

Yes, lone and penniless I stood,
    One bitter winter's morrow,
My household angel pure and good,
    Was left alone in sorrow.

Her only child, her little Fred,
    The flower of three short years,
Lay tossing on his little bed,
    Unconscious of her tears.

With breaking heart, all night alone,
    She watched the waning life ;
And just before the morning's dawn,
    He pass'd from earthly strife.

That self-same night with madden'd brain,
    On drink's wild tempest tost,
I shook the God-curs'd dice again,
    I stak'd my all and lost.

Yes, all was lost, the little bed,
    Where darling Fred had died ;
Where lay in death his curly head,
    All wreck'd on drink's dark tide.

Stung with remorse, o'ercome with shame,
    And wild with poisoned breath,
I thought my darken'd ruin'd fame
    Had better end in death.

I could not meet my homeless wife,
    Nor look on Fred's last sleep ;
Better to end my useless life
    In Linden's quiet deep.

On Linden's bank at last I knelt,
    To breathe one broken prayer,
When fingers soft and light I felt
    Pass gently through my hair.

That fond caress, I knew it well,
    It soothed my burning brain,
And like some wondrous mystic spell,
    Check'd every inward pain.

And as those tender fingers swept
    Across my fever'd brow,
Some angel surely must have wept,
    I feel that tear-drop now.

Then came in tones I knew so well,
    To but one mortal given,
"My poor misguided one farewell,
    I'll wait for thee in heaven."

It needed none to tell me now
    That voice was hushed for ever,
That gentle hand my throbbing brow,
    Would press again, no never.

Yes, she was dead, that last cold whirl
    Of drink's dark seething sorrow,
Had brought my faithful angel girl,
    The dawn of heaven's morrow.

In dreamless slumber, side by side,
    Lay wife and child at rest ;
She, lovely as when first a bride,
    Her boy upon her breast.

One last fond lingering look I gave,
    One last wild frenzied kiss,
Then laid them in this lowly grave
    With all my dreams of bliss.

Ten years have pass'd, yet not one day
    Has fancy failed to bring
That last sad scene of life's dark way,
    On memory's faithful wing.

And ever o'er life's busy swell,
    That angel whisper's given,
"My poor misguided one farewell,
    I'll wait for thee in heaven."

Yes, Ada waits, and if, e'en now,
    I may but be forgiven,
Here, at her humble grave I vow,
    To live for God and heaven.

And should it be as some would say,
    Unerring wisdom's will,
I pray that her pure spirit may
    Yet love and guide me still.

Dear, gentle Ada, teach my soul
    Thy own pure noble life,
Till far beyond death's ceaseless roll,
    I clasp my angel wife.

THE POET'S WREATH.

A SAD STORY.

She was tired and hungry and sad,
    And had walked weary miles through the day,
And her poor aching heart had been glad
    To have met but a friend by the way.

But of all she had passed was not one
    She could claim by this most common tie,
And with courage and strength almost gone,
    She had scarcely a wish but to die

And yet she was young, she was fair,
    Only twenty-three summers had fled,
Since the child of a fond mother's care,
    Life's brightness around her had spread.

But life's changes had taught her young heart
    That all is not sunshine below,
That the lov'd and the loving must part,
    And the best of us sorrow must know.

That mother had languished and died,
    And the orphan had sorrow'd alone,
For in all this cold, bleak world beside,
    Were but few that her young heart had known.

One maiden aunt only was left,
    Who had offered, though much against will,
To the lonely young creature bereft,
    The place of the lost one to fill.

She was one of that class who believe
    'Tis a sin to love mortals below,
And that all who such notions conceive,
    Are in justice condemned to much woe.

A strict and a constant regard
　　For the Church the old lady profess'd,
But the rest of the world she debarred
　　From a share in her glorified rest.

With her, the poor orphan returned,
　　When her final farewell she had said,
And her heart, which for sympathy yearned,
　　Only met with much coldness instead.

Time pass'd, and in passing restored
　　The smiles and the bloom of her youth,
And her soul ever sought and adored
　　The God of all wisdom and truth.

And yet she would not have profess'd
　　That her life was all blameless and true,
Or that Heaven had specially blessed
　　And chosen her one of its few.

She thought it no sin to be kind,
　　Obliging and free unto all,
And the love which no mortal can bind
　　Had answered her lonely heart's call.

One lov'd her whose life like her own,
　　Unlov'd and uncared for had been,
Who much bitter sorrow had known,
　　And little of comfort had seen.

He was no hypocritical saint,
　　Nor worshipped a creed for its name,
And yet not a blemish or taint
　　Ever sullied his pure honest fame.

They lov'd, and as lovers before,
  Have fancied their joys would abound,
So they, from that bright dreamy shore,
  Discerned not the breakers around.

Two years on the bright sunny stream
  They had floated in happy content ;
Two years of a married life's dream
  In blissful repose they had spent.

Then sorrow had broken the spell,
  And darkened their life's sunny sky,
And as wave after wave rose and fell,
  They re-echoed their hearts' bitter cry.

One sweet little gem they had seen
  Pass away at its brightest and best,
Like the beautiful dream that had been
  Ere sorrow had entered their rest.

And now the young early-tried wife
  Had a sorrow much greater in store,
For he whom she loved as her life,
  Would soon in the world be no more.

Consumption, that blight of our land,
  That robs us of earth's fairest flowers,
Had weakened the heart and the hand,
  And numbered his days and his hours.

Long and earnestly, too, had he prayed,
  And struggled to live for her sake,
Till even proud death had delayed,
  As though it were cruel to take.

They had long ago spent their last cent,
   And strangers and friends had been kind,
But of all who had come or had sent,
   The creed-loving aunt was behind.

Their letters unanswered remained,
   Their pleadings for help were in vain,
Till the heart-broken girl had attained
   A state of distraction and pain.

She threw herself wildly beside
   The one she was powerless to save,
And murmured, "Would God we had died
   With the darling now laid in her grave."

Then rousing herself with a start,
   And clasping the dearly loved form,
She whispered, "Take courage, dear heart,
   We shall meet beyond reach of the storm."

Then calling a friend to her side,
   She calmly informed her that now,
No matter how wild ran the tide,
   To the course of events she would bow.

She would start for her aunt's in that hour,
   If she but consented to stay,
And surely some unforeseen power
   Would move all her sternness away.

But when her "good-bye" she would say
   To the one for whose sake she had striven,
Her newly-found courage gave way,
   'Twas so hard from his side to be driven.

One moment she wavered and felt
    That nothing could tempt her to leave ;
The next she instinctively knelt,
    Entreating he would not thus grieve.

" I will not be long from your side,
    But something, you know, must be done ;
All other fair means have I tried,
    And nothing remains but this one.

I mean to get something for you,
    For I know that you suffer from want,
Besides, dear, the rent is quite due,
    And your covering sadly too scant.

My aunt has enough and to spare,
    Her income no little one is,
Then why should I want for a share ?
    Or why should I suffer like this ?

I think when she looks upon me,
    How weary, how worn, and how spent,
She cannot a Christian be,
    If her heart does not softly relent."

He tried in his weak feeble way,
    Her purpose to change, and replied,
"Don't leave me, my darling, I pray,
    For I fear that some ill might betide.

'Tis six weary miles by the way,
    Too much for your strength I am sure,
Then, dearest one, stay with me, stay,
    For your absence I could not endure."

Again, did she linger and wait,
   And soothe him by kindly caress,
And again, while her courage seemed great,
   Did she murmur a loving "God bless."

And tearing herself from his side
   Reluctantly hastened away,
And the cold bitter winds she defied,
   They were powerless her footsteps to stay.

On, on, through the streets and the lanes,
   Impell'd by a love strong as death,
Still on, till she wearily gains
   The home where she drew her first breath.

She would gladly have rested awhile,
   Within sight of her once happy home,
But there yet remained two weary mile
   That her poor aching feet must yet roam.

'Twas there we had seen her pass by,
   So tired and hungry and sad,
With scarcely a wish but to die,
   For her heart nevermore could be glad.

She entered at length through the gate
   Of the home where so lately she dwelt,
And stern and unflinching as fate,
   She checked the wild fear that she felt.

Her timid and scarcely heard knock
   Was answered by one she well knew,
Whose heart seemed encased in a rock,
   While her look pierced her tender heart through

The cold cruel words that then fell
    From this meek hypocritical saint,
'Twould serve no good purpose to tell,
    Neither care I her virtues to paint.

'Tis enough that I know she refused
    To receive the poor girl for a night,
Then to church she went airing her views,
    Proud to think she had done what was right.

In the meantime her neice had been found,
    Overcome by fatigue and distress,
On the hard and unpitying ground,
    In a state which demanded redress.

She had fainted from weakness and pain,
    From over-exertion and cold,
And 'twas doubtful if ever again
    Those lips would her sorrows unfold.

Kind hearts bore her back to the home
    From which she had lately been driven
Nevermore from its threshold to roam
    Till she passed to the threshold of heaven.

When from church the old lady returned,
    And understood all that had passed,
Her creed-loving conscience was turned
    To its long-despised duty at last.

She saw what a hollow pretence
    Her boasted religion had been,
And vowed that for ever from hence,
    The fruit of her life should be seen.

She left not the side of her niece,
   As she lay through the long weary night,
Unconsciously dreaming of peace
   And talking with angels of light.

Once only her memory came
   Like a gleam from some far sunny land,
And softly she murmured the name
   For which she had pledged heart and hand.

Once only a beautiful smile,
   Which the watchers will never forget,
Played o'er her fair features awhile,
   And chased every shade of regret.

Once only her gentle voice broke
   On the ears of the friends who had met,
But the few loving words that she spoke
   Are echoes of memory yet.

She spoke not of ills that were past,
   Nor troubles that soon would be o'er,
But of pleasures that ever shall last,
   Beyond this, our earth's dreary shore.

Of the poor, weeping aunt she implored
   That she would not herself so distress,
For that God, whom the angels adored,
   Her earth-wearied spirit would bless.

Then breathing a prayer for the one
   Who soon would rejoin her again,
'Ere fell the last word, she was gone,
   And free from all sorrow and pain.

They brought the poor husband with care,
    And tenderly told him the truth,
While he murmured but one simple prayer,
    To rejoin the lov'd friend of his youth.

Once only he looked on the face
    Of his once happy blooming young wife,
And a smile which no sorrow could chase
    Revealed a new dawning of life.

He uttered no needless farewell,
    But quietly passed from her side,
And ere the next morning rays fell,
    He, too, had rejoicingly died.

Together they laid them to rest,
    With the darling who passed from their sight,
And who shall deny they are blest
    In the realms of celestial light?

And now my sad story is told,
    And this lesson to me it would teach,
If the name of a Christian we hold,
    We must practice the virtues we preach.

THE SUICIDE'S GRAVE.

Judge him not, O mortal man,
Leave him with the God who can,
Dare not, righteous though ye be,
Judgment pass on such as he.

Judge him not, ye ne'er can know,
E'er he struck the fatal blow,
E'er he took his life away,
How far reason held her sway.

Judge him not, he once was free,
Once could boast as well as ye,
Once respected was by all,
Friend, beware, ye too might fall.

Judge him not, ye ne'er can tell
How he struggl'd ere he fell,
How that heart, now cold and still,
Wrestl'd with impending ill.

True he sinn'd, and deeply too,
So have I, pray, have not you?
Guilty all, Oh then who can
Dare to judge his fellow man.

Have ye not a thought to spare
For an aged father's care?
One whose heart is bow'd with grief,
Would ye tender no relief?

Could ye not at least restrain
Cruel words, that only pain?
If ye can no comfort give,
Let at least his memory live.

Think of what he was at best,
In his grave inter the rest;
Let his funeral shadow fall
O'er his faults and failings all.

MY CHILDHOOD'S HOME.

(ON SEEING IT DEMOLISHED.)

Ye might have spared my childhood's home,
    That long remember'd spot
That wheresoe'er on earth I roam,
    Will never be forgot.
Smile not because those walls are dear,
    More dear than words can tell,
Nor deem me weak if, with a tear,
    I bid them now farewell.

'Twas only there I knew the love,
    That comes but once in life,
Which streams from purer realms above,
    Beyond earth's weary strife.
There only for a few short years
    That gentle mother led;
And there I wept my first sad tears
    For that lov'd mother dead.

To me those walls re-echo yet
    The songs of eventide,
When father, sisters, brothers met
    There by our ain fireside;
Each well-loved form I watch again
    As one by one they sever,
Oh! memory, 'tis a bitter pain,
    To know they're gone for ever.

'Twas there the muse first taught my soul
    To try her feeble strings,
And soar beyond earth's busy roll
    On bright poetic wings;

To gather from celestial bowers
    Those richer gems of thought,
Which often in life's darkest hours
    Have sweetest comfort brought.

Though fairer scenes may charm awhile
    As through the world I roam,
I'd pledge them all with but a smile
    For thee my childhood's home;
But tears are vain, and I must bow
    With feelings none may tell,
I bid thee, and for ever now,
    A final sad farewell.

LEOPOLD, DUKE OF ALBANY.

IN MEMORIAM.

He is not dead! oh! no, not dead,
    Though pass'd beyond our mortal sight;
That well-trained spirit has but fled
    Back to its home in realms of light.

He is not dead; oh! no, not dead;
    'Tis but the mortal scene is o'er;
That life shall still its lustre shed,
    And reach us from the brighter shore.

He is not dead; oh! no, not dead,
    But only dropped the worn-out clay;
While he, by angel guardians led,
    Has reached the home for which we pray.

He is not dead ; oh ! no, not dead ;
   Such heaven-born goodness cannot die ;
The path in which he lov'd to tread
   Leads on to life beyond the sky.

He is not gone ; oh ! no, not gone,
   For ever from the lov'd one's side ;
Affection's flower shall still bloom on
   In richer soil, beyond the tide.

And though the mortal eye may fail
   To trace the loving presence near,
We know that those beyond the veil
   Can oft our drooping spirits cheer.

That life of promise bright and fair
   Can not in funeral gloom have set :
Intelligence so rich and rare,
   Can lend its ray to mortals yet.

That loving soul that sought to bless
   The homes of this his honoured land,
Still loves and labours none the less
   That England's sons yet free may stand.

That soul of music's richest vein,
   That now can join the angels' song,
Shall echo back some loftier strain,
   To cheer earth's restless weary throng.

Then dream not that his life is o'er,
   While but the mortal stage is run ;
For on the bright celestial shore,
   His real life is but begun.

And voices on the silent air
   Float o'er us by sweet echoes led,
And whisper to the mourner's prayer,
   " He is not dead ! oh no, not dead ! "

PITY ME NOT.

In a recent discussion on the merits and demerits of eternal torment, I was asked why I could not believe in the doctrine. I replied that the eternal duration of punishment seemed to me very unjust, and that a righteous, holy, and wise God could never have so ordained it. I was very much pitied, one friend observing that he was very sorry for me. To that friend I dedicate these few lines.

Pity me not ! It were pity indeed,
Did I preach to the world such a merciless creed ;
Did I own that a God whom I love and adore,
Would assign any soul such a fate evermore.

Pity me not ! That I dare to rebel
'Gainst the terrible creed of your favourite hell ;
That I dare to renounce such a cruel decree,
As unworthy that mercy, so boundless and free.

Pity me not ! That I cannot consent
To join in the dirge of your hopeless lament ;
To that doctrine, as yet, this most obstinate pen,
Refuses to sign an eternal Amen.

That sin must be punished, I freely admit,
But in judgment on others, are you fit to sit ?
Have your lives been so holy, so spotless and true,
That the fate of a world must be ordered by you ?

Oh! if it were thus, I might tremble indeed,
What a doom would be mine for denouncing your creed!
For teaching the power of the publican's prayer,
Instead of the wail of eternal despair.

But conscious am I that the One whom I trust,
Whose laws are unchangeable, perfect and just,
In His infinite wisdom, could never decree,
That a soul's retribution eternal should be.

And if, as you intimate, some time I may
Find out that in this I've mistaken my way;
If, for preaching of mercy to weak erring men,
I am sent to perdition, oh! pity me then!

SONG—THE DRUNKARD'S DYING CHILD.

Dear father, come stay with your darling,
    Poor mother is weary and sad,
All day she has wept as she nursed me,
    And call'd me her poor dying lad.
Yes, father, 'tis true I am dying,
    And something I'm wishful to say,
'Tis only this night I'll be with you,
    To-morrow I'll be far away.

CHORUS:

Yes, father, I'm going away,
    Oh, promise your poor dying lad,
That always at home you will stay,
    When mother is lonely and sad.

THE POET'S WREATH.

My father, I would not distress you,
    Or cause you one moment of pain,
But, oh, 'tis a joy to behold you,
    My own sober father again,
Just lay my poor head on your bosom,
    And call me your darling once more,
And again I will pray that I meet you
    On a brighter and happier shore.

        CHORUS: Yes, father, &c.

Nay, weep not so bitterly, father,
    Nor call the Good Saviour unkind,
This seeming unkindness will bring you
    A blessing some day you will find.
And oh, if it be but permitted,
    And teacher says surely it will,
I'll ask the good angels to bring me
    To show you I'm loving you still.

        CHORUS: Yes, father, &c.

And now I am just a bit tired,
    I'll lay on my pillow and rest,
And mother will sit close beside me,
    And sing of the realms of the blest.
How soothing, how sweet, and how cheering,
    What beauties bewilder my sight—
Dear father, dear mother, I'm going,
    Come, kiss me a loving "Good night."

        CHORUS: Yes, father, &c.

SONG—THE FATHER'S VOW.

No, they can never tempt me now :
   The wild mad dream is o'er :
Here, at this little grave, I vow
   To be a man once more.
Oh could I call the bitter past
   Back from oblivion's deep ;
Life's closing shades might wrap me then
   In death's cold dreamless sleep.

      Life's wasted hours I would recall,
         But no, they're gone for ever ;
      Their golden promises will bloom
         For me again, no, never.

What bitter memories throng my brain,
   As fancy wakes the past :
What loving forms I see again,
   Too bright, too fair, to last.
What blissful hours of holy joy,
   What richest treasures lost :
Oh drink ! thy gaudy gilded toy,
   Has been a bitter cost.
      Life's wasted hours, &c.

But tears are vain, the past is fled,
   With all its trifl'd hours :
The present but remains instead
   To test my waning powers.
But He, who heard my Willie pray
   That I might sober be,
Will surely send some angel friend,
   To teach and comfort me.
      Life's wasted hours, &c.

Dear Willie, is thy spirit near,
   And can'st thou hear me now?
It must thy loving spirit cheer,
   To know my sacred vow.
Yes, darling one, thy prayer is heard,
   Henceforth I will be free,
And live a life that's sure to bring,
   My spirit home to thee.
      Life's wasted hours, &c.

TO THE MEMORY OF THE LIFEBOAT CREW.

HONOUR THE BRAVE.

Honour the brave-hearted heroic band,
Who dashed through the waves at stern duty's command,
Nobly they died in their efforts to save,
Then honour, proud England, thy martyrs so brave.

Honour the brave, 'mid your festival cheer,
Check the wild mirth with true sympathy's tear,
Hark! o'er the dark cruel merciless wave
Comes the echo of thousands: "We honour your brave."

Honour the brave in your annals of fame,
With loving remembrance encircle their name,
Bring nature's rich tributes to deck the lone grave,
And with all that is beautiful honour the brave.

Honour the brave who have dared to be true,
Who have honoured their country so gloriously too;
Let Englishmen ever on land or on wave,
Be true to their manhood and honour the brave.

For oh! not alone are they honour'd on earth,
But surely by those of a happier birth,
For we hear from beyond the cold pitiless grave
Some angel voice whisper, *We honour the brave.*

A PLEA FOR THE UNEMPLOYED.

Work, work, work,
   Is the cry throughout England to-day,
From thousands of earth's noble sons
   Who are wearily plodding life's way :
Morn, noon, and at night they are found,
   Still pleading for work and for bread,
But often still heavier bound,
   By scorn or cold pity instead.

Poor toilers, they ever are willing
   To live by the sweat of their brow,
So proud of a dearly earn'd shilling,
   E'en that is forbidden them now.
Homes once the fond pride of a mother,
   And joy of a lov'd father's heart,
Now pass to the care of another,
   And lov'd ones are drifting apart.

Strong hearts are now bending with sorrow
   For dear ones around them unfed,
As every succeeding to-morrow,
   Still echoes, "No work and no bread."
Poor mothers look on in their anguish,
   Unnerved by the dark cruel tide,
And bright little innocents languish,
   And some have e'en famished and died.

Brave hearts have encountered much danger,
   And buried the hopes of bright years,
And sought in the land of the stranger,
   Relief from their torturing fears.
How many who cross'd the wide ocean,
   From ruin some lov'd one to save,
Have found for their noble devotion
   A home in the strangers' cold grave.

Oh! who shall foretell the dark sorrows,
   Fast shading our own belov'd land,
Dark days, but still darker to-morrows,
   Seem threatening on every hand.
Oh! England, the home of my fathers,
   The land of the brave and the free,
What dark desolation now gathers,
   My once happy country, o'er thee.

Rouse! Englishmen, rouse to your duty,
   Arrest the mad pitiless wave,
Save England's proud genius and beauty,
   From want and a premature grave.
Oh! hear ye of might and of power,
   The prayer of this desolate band,
And save in their bitterest hour
   The hard-toiling sons of your land.

In the name of the heavens above you,
   In the name of the mercy ye plead,
In the name of the angels who love you,
   They ask you to pity their need.
In the name of the blessings that greet you,
   By which you are sheltered and fed,
In the name of the God who must meet you,
   They ask you for work and for bread.

ONE BY ONE

One by one they are passing away,
Leaving fond hearts fill'd with grief and dismay,
Teaching a lesson we loathe yet to learn :
Back to our Mother Earth all must return.

One by one little graves may be seen,
Hiding the form of some bright fairy queen,
Lovingly tended and planted with care :
Ah, Death ! who shall tell us what treasures lie there ?

One by one see the empty wee chairs,
Where lately they whispered their innocent prayers,
While borne on the breeze with the evening's soft light,
Comes the last whispered sound of our darling's "Good
    Night."

One by one from our schools they are gone,
With lessons unfinished or scarce yet begun,
While the playmates assemble 'mid silence profound,
And the death of the lov'd one is whispered around.

One by one they are joining the ranks
Of the thousands assembled on Jordan's fair banks :
While the angels so lovingly, tenderly true,
Are training, oh, Mothers ! those children for you.

Then leave them in care of those beings so kind ;
Not one shall be lost—no, not one left behind,
But when earth-life with you shall be over and gone,
They'll give back your jewels they took one by one.

NO CREED.

What a noise in our day about teaching the way
    To a better and holier life ;
What bitter dissent among preachers to-day,
    What jealousy, anger, and strife.
What pride, and unholy contention for creed,
    What a craze for distinction and fame ;
'Twould astound the whole realm of perdition indeed,
    This great theological shame.

What wonder the poor, scatter'd sheep should be lost,
    While the shepherds dispute by the way ;
On a sea of religious upheavings they're toss't,
    And thousands are drifting astray,
While they who profess to be chosen to lead,
    And teach us life's duties as well,
Are warmly contending on dogmas and creed,
    And whether or no there's a hell.

They stand on their trial, grave charges are laid,
    And the world is alive to the fact—
That the proof of religion for which they are paid,
    Their lives have most shamefully lack'd.
They have rous'd opposition, dissension, and strife,
    By a love of pounds, shillings, and pence ;
Would God they would show us more practical life,
    And less of self-righteous pretence.

Had they faithfully taught a free Gospel of love ;
    Had their lives been as pure as they might ;
Had their thoughts and affections but centr'd above ;
    Had their minds been receptive of light ;

Had they taught only Christ and His beautiful life,
    Irrespective of party or creed,
Instead of a world of injustice and strife,
    His Name had been honour'd indeed.

That Name they have slighted, dishonoured, and laid
    In the scale of self-interest and pride ;
Expecting all wrong to be cancell'd and paid
    By simply believing He died.
Forgetting He liv'd an example to all,
    Of equity, justice, and right ;
Forgetting, alas! His entreaty and call,
    To walk as the children of light.

That life of undying, illustrious fame
    Sheds a halo o'er earth's dreary way,
Which still through the sin-clouds of darkness and shame
    Leads on to a happier day.
Teach this, and religion shall gain her lost power ;
    Teach this, and the world shall be free ;
Teach this, and poor mortals shall dread not the hour
    That sets the earth-wearied one free.

Talk less about hell and a terrible God,
    Tell us more of His glories above ;
All nature declares Him from cloudlet to sod
    A Being of wonderful love.
The beauty, the grace, the harmonious blend
    Of systems and forces that gather
Around and above us, all gloriously tend
    To unite us in one common Father.

Then cease your dissension and take a survey
    Of nature's grand volume around ;
In her wonders by night, or her glories by day,
    No jarring or discord is found.

No threat on her unsullied page can we read,
　No anger or hatred whatever,
But proof most abundant, yea, more than we need,
　Of a God that will love us for ever.

REVERIE WRITTEN IN OAK HILL GROUNDS.

'Tis sweet at the hour of twilight to roam
Through the grounds of this loved and once beautiful home:
To gaze on the glories of nature around,
And rest in the stillness so deep and profound.

'Tis sweet to reflect 'mid the solitude here,
With no one to check me or chide the fond tear;
With none to condemn me as foolish and weak,
Because I would rather such loneliness seek.

Here, all undisturbed, I may linger awhile,
Secure from the world's cruel censure or smile;
Away from its cold, bitter, treacherous scorn,
I can dream of a brighter and happier morn.

Yes, dream of a fairer and holier day,
When this life and its cares shall be all pass'd away;
Where names of distinction no longer are shown,
But the soul by its harvest of fruits shall be known.

Then cease, weary heart, let thy murmurings rest,
Remember none here are exclusively blest;
All things that surround me are doom'd to decay,
And the sorrows that press me are passing away.

This mansion before me now silent and drear,
To some hearts I have known was once sacredly dear :
'Twas the home of a Christian lady who trod
If mortal e'er could, in the paths of her God.

These walls have re-echoed a fond Mother's prayer,
And witness'd a father's devotion and care :
While the innocent gambols of childhood have lent
A mystical charm to its air of content.

These beautiful walks have been press'd by the tread
Of fairy-like forms which now rank with the dead,
And the dying leaves falling around at my feet,
Make the wild desolation more sad and complete.

This willow so gracefully drooping would seem
To be faithfully guarding some beautiful dream ;
Perhaps, if a voice in its leaves could be found,
They would echo some lover's fond whisper around.

Here's the grave of poor Floe, who has long pass'd away,
But whose true canine nature is honoured to-day ;
And a beautiful thought his lone grave might suggest,
So to live, that another might honour our rest.

This Rosary once was a favourite spot,
Which some who yet live can have never forgot,
With its wealth of the rarest and costliest kind,
That the eye of a critical florist might find.

Now little remains of its grandeur and pride,
And that little but waits the return of the tide ;
Soon all will have pass'd on times hurrying stream,
And nothing remain but fond Memory's dream.

Once, noble and beautiful home, I would pray
That some one would save thee from further decay,
Would bring back thy glory and pride as of old,
I would, if my wishes could furnish the gold.

But then, if thou still must pass on to decay,
If none will yet care for thee, surely, I may,
Thou shalt teach me in mute silent eloquence still,
For I love thee, though fallen, once Noble Oak Hill.

IN MEMORIAM.

MRS. SMITH, Spring Hill.

My best adviser mid life's perplexing cares, my sympathising friend and counsellor in sorrow's hour, to whom I owe what only the light of eternity can reveal, when we shall understand more clearly the force and beauty of those oft forgotten words—"As ye sow ye shall also reap."

One Angel less on earth,
But one more gem in heaven,
Another soul at rest—
Long toss'd and tempest driven;
Another barque has anchor'd
Safe in the port of bliss,
Another saint has enter'd
A better life than this.

Another light has left us,
To deck some fairer sky,
Another long-tried Christian
Has taught us how to die;

Another noble spirit
Has laid life's burden down,
And over death triumphant
Now wears the victor's crown.

And, oh! let no one chide me,
If here I dare to say,
A better, purer spirit
Has seldom pass'd away.
Earth holds but few so fitted
Youth's faltering steps to guide,
Or in life's darkest sorrow
To find some brighter side.

With tenderest acts of mercy,
With brightest gems of thought,
With saintlike true devotion,
Her mortal life was fraught.
And now in calm submission,
We, who have known her best,
Can praise the God who gives her
A well-earn'd heaven of rest.

Thou dear enfranchised spirit,
My counsellor and friend,
To emulate thy goodness
Shall be my aim and end.
The seeds of Christian duty
I'll guard with zealous care,
Till, in that world of beauty,
I reap an harvest fair.

SONG OF THE WEARY.

Yes, I am weary of waiting,
　Waiting for sunnier days;
Weary, yes, weary of sorrow,
　Of life and its dark giddy maze.
Weary of watching for sunshine,
　And grasping but shadows instead,
And weary, oh, weary of hoping
　For joys that for ever are fled.

　　　CHORUS—Oh life, weary life,
　　　　　　　No rest is in thee,
　　　　　　Far away from thy strife
　　　　　　　I would I were free.

Weary of trusting to friendship,
　The friendship of happier days,
In all the dark sorrows that press me,
　I see no familiar face.
Weary of empty profession,
　Of gilded position and name.
Life seems but a race and a struggle
　For honour, distinction, and fame.

　　　CHORUS—"Oh life, weary life," &c.

Oh, is there no happier region?
　No world of probation but this?
No life where we take up the footsteps
　Which here by the way we may miss?
No home of the poor oppress'd spirit,
　Where justice, unerring, may dwell?
Oh, surely some angel of mercy
　Of such a sweet refuge can tell.

　　　CHORUS—"Oh life, weary life," &c.

They speak of a rest for the weary,
   Somewhere in God's mansions above,
They sing of His wonderful mercy,
   And call Him a Father of love.
A Father, then sure I may trust Him,
   He'll do what is kindest and best,
I'll wait till this life shall be over,
   And then I shall joyously rest.
        Chorus—"Oh life, weary life," &c.

SONG OF HOPE.

Poor earth-wearied mourner, despair not,
   Though dreary and dark be the way,
Above the deep sorrows that bind thee
   There lingers one comforting ray ;
One star which no gloom can o'ershadow,
   One gem of celestial light,
One beam from the sunnier regions,
   Where skies are unclouded and bright.
     Chorus—Rest, weary one, rest,
         Hope's comforting ray
       Leads faithfully on
         To a happier day.

Though friendship once cherished forsake thee,
   And dearer ones learn to forget,
And in the dense darkness around thee,
   The sun of thy life seems to set ;
Remember the dawn ever chaseth
   The longest and dreariest night,
And the shadows that darken thy pathway
   Must yield to the dawning of light.
        Chorus—"Rest, weary one, rest," &c.

Oh, yes, there are worlds of probation,
  And happier regions of bliss,
And a beautiful rest for the pilgrim,
  Whose footsteps are weary in this :
A home of repose for the spirit
  Borne down by oppressions of earth,
Where justice knows not the distinction
  Of honour, position, or birth.
        CHORUS—" Rest, weary one, rest," &c.

Then look from the trials around thee,
  Beyond and above the dark swell,
And know that a Father who loves thee
  Hath ordered all wisely and well.
Yes, trust such a Parent of Mercy
  To do what is kindest and best,
And when this earth life shall be over
  Thy soul shall rejoice in His rest.
        CHORUS—" Rest, weary one, rest," &c.

CAN THIS BE TRUE.

"There are two hundred million Christians on the earth."—DR. TALMAGE.

Two hundred million Christians !
  Can any one believe it ?
Would all the fallen sons of men
  As gospel truth receive it ?
Will listening saints and angels hear
  Unmov'd this declaration ?
No, Doctor, no, for once you clear
  All bounds of moderation.

THE POET'S WREATH.

If this were true, our world would not
    Be steep'd in sin and sorrow ;
Nor thousand suffering toilers dread
    The dawn of each to-morrow.
No proud oppressor then would stand
    With foot upon his brother ;
And boast of adding land to land,
    By trampling on another.

If this were true, no hungry bands
    Of unemploy'd would meet us ;
Nor mute appealing stricken looks
    Of starving children greet us.
The river would not hide so much
    Proud intellect and beauty ;
If half your Christians lived as such,
    And nobly did their duty.

If this were true, this fearful swell
    Of impure life around us,
Had never reached this awful pass
    To utterly confound us.
Life had not been to thousand hearts
    One scene of toil and sorrow ;
While scarce one ray of hope imparts
    A light o'er death's dark morrow.

Two hundred million ! most I fear
    Are only such in name ;
And bitterly denounced by One
    Of everlasting fame.
He wreath'd the Christian's holy brow
    With loving acts of duty ;
And woe to those who dare to now
    Disgrace its heavenly beauty.

Professing Christians stand to-day
  Condemn'd by earth and heaven;
The saving of a beauteous world
  Into their charge was given.
And how have they betray'd the trust?
  For answer look around you;
And sin's wild deluge surely must
  Most utterly astound you.

Supposing Jesus came to-day,
  Just to inspect your mission:
How few who proudly boast His Name
  Could stand His supervision.
While few indeed could bring the sheaves
  From Christian lives of beauty;
Thousands would bring but faded leaves,
  Types of neglected duty.

Would He believe this ruin'd world
  Did credit to the teaching
Of all those million souls who prate
  Of saving Gospel preaching?
Would He believe this fearful blight,
  This tide of sorrow's tears
Could follow on the Gospel light
  Of eighteen hundred years?

No, Doctor, no, your boast I fear
  Sounds much like idle ranting;
The proof of what you boldly state,
  The world is sadly wanting.
We judge the trees by what we see,
  And prove from nature's teaching,
They only honest Christians be
  Who practice what they're preaching.

Then turn your Christians out to work
   In God's wide field of labour ;
Bid every man and woman too,
   Be honest to their neighbour.
Bid every poor down-trodden slave
   Whose lives are scar'd and blighted ;
No longer kneel to man and crave
   For justice scorn'd and slighted.

Bid every tyrant snap the chain
   He's forg'd around his brother ;
And cease to reap ungodly gain
   By crushing down another.
Bid him restore while yet he may
   The spoils of base oppression ;
Or dare not on his soul to pray
   Or boast a saint's profession.

Go bid your Christian tyrants learn
   From Matthew twenty-third,
The woes denounced by Christ on such,
   Most bitter then were heard.
And would He find less cause to-day
   'Mid all earth's desolation ;
Though million Christians daily pray
   To see the world's salvation ?

Go turn your Christians in the slums
   Those dens of sin and sorrow ;
And bid them cheer some hopeless ones
   And brighten some dark morrow.
Bid them raise up some little one
   To childhood's life and beauty ;
And win some erring fallen one
   Back to their God and duty.

Go send them to the toiler's home,
  Where children cry for bread :
And bid them cheer the fainting heart
  And raise the drooping head.
Go draft them to the sufferer's side,
  Though poison'd streams may roll :
'Tis their's, whatever may betide,
  To stand beside the soul.

In short, go tell your Christians all
  To live Christ's beauteous life ;
To open earth's sweet springs of joy,
  And stem her fearful strife.
Do this, and stay the angel hand,
  Now writing Ichabod,
Do this, and save your native land
  And glorify your God.

IMPROMPTU ON PRIMROSE DAY.

TO THE MEMORY OF LORD BEACONSFIELD.

Honour your Statesman ! ye friends of the blue,
To his long rever'd memory be faithful and true ;
Heed not, though the battle rage fiercely and long,
Stand firm and unflinching, your Union is strong.

Honour your Statesman ! by all that is pure,
Whose life no political shade can obscure ;
Whose life like some radiant beacon of light,
Gleams brightest and best through the darkness of night.

Honour your Statesman! though passed from your view—
He lives, but a life more transcendently true;
Death does not the bond of true sympathy sever,
'Tis the link that shall bind us in union for ever.

Honour your Statesman! by honest endeavour,
All strife and dissension to banish for ever;
Lost peace and contentment with justice restore,
Till the cry of oppression is heard of no more.

Honour your Statesman! by noble ambition,
To stem the wild torrent of proud opposition;
By the spirit in which he once manfully stood,
And calmly assured them that hear him they should.

Honour your Statesman! and take up the strain,
Borne back by the wavelets of time once again;
And the prophetic force of his sentiments spoken,
The future shall tell by a Union unbroken.

Honour your Statesman! your freedom demands it,
Rouse to your duty, your Maker commands it;
Peace to your country, your Queen, and your God,
Is the cry that resoundeth from cloudlet to sod.

Honour your Statesman! whom none could excel,
Whose loss to his country no Angel can tell:
Though dead he shall live in our annals of fame,
And England for ever be proud of his name.

THE RIGHT HON. W. E. GLADSTONE,

ON HIS SEVENTY-NINTH BIRTHDAY, DECEMBER 29TH, 1888.

" Hail, Gladstone !" all hail to the time-honour'd day
That saw thy barque launch'd upon life's stormy way,
That witnessed thy star, lit by wisdom divine,
Burst forth 'mid the gems of creation to shine.

Though storms of wild fury thy barque have assail'd,
Heaven-born is thy courage, that never yet fail'd,
Though clouds of thick darkness have swept o'er thy sky,
" Still on," was thy watchword, to conquer or die.

Many wrecks have passed by thee on life's cruel tide,
Which well might deter one less tempted and tried :
But wrecks, nor yet breakers, nor rocks could appal,
Thou hast mann'd the boat well, thou hast breasted them all.

And fain would we wish in the sunset of life
Thy soul might have rest from the conflict and strife,
That crown'd with the laurels so gloriously won,
Thy future days might have been peacefully run.

But no ; the world needs thee, rest cometh not now,
Though silver'd thy locks and care-furrow'd thy brow,
Once more the storm gathers, fierce, thickly, and fast,
Once more thou must fight, but we pray 'tis the last

On, then, noble champion, true-hearted and brave,
To the rescue of those who have pray'd thee to save,
Trust God for all counsel and wisdom to guide,
Nor dread for the issue, Heaven's court shall decide.

Thy footprints are telling on life's busy way,
And rousing to action the youth of our day,
The life thou hast lived so devotedly well,
Years hence in the world shall its influence tell.

And oh, what a joy must be thine at the last,
When earth with its trials of state shall be past ;
With the harvest before thee most gloriously won,
And the Master's proud welcome, Most Faithfully done.

Then hail to our statesman, so valiant and true,
Of such noble England can boast but a few ;
A friend to his country, his Queen, and his God,
Let Gladstone re-echo from cloudlet to sod.

MOTHER'S BOY.

A mother deprived of her heart's dearest joy,
Lamenting the loss of her idolized boy :
Alone in her chamber, alone with her God,
Her heart almost broke by this stroke of His rod.

She weeps as she thinks of the joys that are fled,
Fond hopes rudely blighted the hopeful one dead ;
Poor heart now so lonely, how welcome were death,
Thrice welcome to one of such comfort bereft.

Night's shades gather round her, but still she sits there,
Nor yet can her soul find its solace in prayer ;
In heart-broken anguish with lowly bent head,
She murmurs the name of her beautiful dead.

Why say we of those whom God takes to His rest—
Why say we they're dead, when with life they are blest?
Immortal and sinless, transcendently pure,
A deathless existence, eternal and sure.

When the tempest of grief o'er that lone heart had passed,
And the soul bursts the bonds that had bound her at last,
When the trembling heart whispered, "O, Father, I pray,
Teach me to submit to Thy all-righteous sway."

A calm like the lulling of nature to sleep
Soothes the mother's worn heart, and she ceases to weep;
A voice lov'd and loving breathes tenderly sweet,
"Mourn not, dearest mother, ere long we shall meet.

You taught my young heart its first lessons of love,
You told me of angels and mansions above;
The Bible you taught me to love and to read,
And, mother, your labour is blessed indeed.

In my home with the angels now safely at rest,
'Neath their care and protection most tenderly blest;
Your heart need not fear for me, dangers are o'er,
Temptation and sin can beset me no more.

Then rejoice, dearest mother, and cease to repine,
Your lot might be wept o'er, but, surely, not mine;
You're still in a world of temptation and care,
But fear not, press onward, you'll conquer by prayer.

And, mother, I'll watch you; think not I forget,
Though an angel in heaven, I'm mother's boy yet;
I'll guide you, and guard you, and whisper of rest,
Till you join me again in the realms of the blest."

The mother was comforted, darkness was gone,
Hope's star o'er her pathway shone cheeringly on ;
She saw that her Saviour in mercy had smiled,
As He took to His bosom her beautiful child.

OUR CEMETERY.

What memories awake as we gaze on this scene ;
What fond recollections of those that have been ;
What mingl'd emotions of pleasure and pain—
As fancy recalls us our lov'd ones again.

We see them once more as in life's sunny day,
And fondly we linger o'er scenes passed away ;
We hear the lov'd voices, remember'd so well,
And listen again to their dying farewell.

Ah! yes we remember, we ne'er can forget,
When our aching hearts murmur'd " O Father, not yet."
When we pray'd death to spare us our joy and our pride,
He turn'd coldly from us and smil'd, as they died.

Proud monarch, pale tyrant, we own thy vast sway ;
We know that nought earthly thy arrows can stay ;
Our fairest and loveliest, brightest and best,
Pass away from the homes they have gladden'd and blest.

Thou hast robb'd us of fathers most sacredly dear—
Of mothers whose presence could comfort and cheer ;
While the dearly lov'd sister so joyous and bright,
With the brave-hearted brother have pass'd from our sight.

Thou hast call'd the young husband, in manhood's full glow;
The blooming young bride at thy bidding must go ;
E'en the babes we have cherish'd and nurtured with care—
No tears, no entreaties, could move thee to spare.

Their bright little heads are laid low at our feet ;
We linger and wait almost hoping to meet —
Nay, longing to snatch from the cold cheerless grave
The darling young forms we had pray'd thee to save.

We pray'd thee, but ah ! did we know what we ask,
Should we plead that their winning smiles longer might last?
Did we see all their trials, temptations, and care,
Methinks we should never entreat thee to spare.

Could we gaze on the home where our little ones dwell,
More joyous than poets or sages can tell.
Most tenderly guarded by angels' fond care,
Our hearts would re-echo 'tis well they are there.

'Tis well they are there, then, mothers, prepare,
He'll give back your treasures more blooming and fair ;
If faithful to Him who has call'd them away,
Your joy will be greater at some future day.

Earth is not our home : Heaven may be at last,
When trials and troubles and dangers are past.
Oh ! then we shall know, and in knowing be blest,
That these farewells of earth have been all for the best.

SHIPWRECK'D.

"In the midst of life we are in death."

Words full of meaning and painfully true,
Dying without even love's fond adieu;
Smiling one moment in beauty and life,
Plung'd the next instant in death's cruel strife.

Fathers of little ones left to bewail,
Mothers whose cries make the stoutest heart fail,
Brothers and sisters in life's early morn,
From hearts that would shield them are ruthlessly torn.

No pity has death on the newly-made bride,
Or the darling young cherub, some fond mother's pride;
The heart's dearest treasures she cares not to save,
But lays the lov'd forms in a watery grave.

Oh, ye who have wept at the grave of the fair,
And thought it a cruel affliction to bear;
Reflect for one moment on scenes such as this,
Then your case will most surely seem temper'd with bliss.

Your lov'd ones have died 'neath your own tender care,
Consol'd and upheld by your own loving prayer;
While their last happy words have rejoiced your fond heart,
"In heaven we'll meet where no sorrows can part."

But here no fond look or a token of love,
Not even the welcome, "We'll meet you above;"
The heart that so late with affection had thrill'd,
'Neath the cold cruel waters for ever is still'd.

Ah, death! Thou art mighty; thy conquests are great;
No offers can tempt thee one moment to wait;
Though breaking hearts pray thee their lov'd ones to spare,
In vain—all in vain—is their agoniz'd prayer.

What homes thou hast robb'd of their joy and their light,
What beautiful forms thou hast hid from our sight;
What fond hopes lay wither'd, what bright joys are fled,
What treasures lay buried—what lov'd ones are dead!

Sweet guardian spirits! oh, say, can ye tell,
With our beautiful dead may we hope it is well?
'Neath your kind loving care do they happily roam?
Do they bask in the bliss of your beautiful home?

Oh, yes, there be surely some happier sphere,
Where all shall be plain that so puzzles us here;
Where the lost shall be found, be it land or by sea,
For all shall be gathered, kind Father, with Thee.

AN APPEAL.

[On the Moorfield Explosion.]

Once again we must turn to our annals of sorrow,
But where shall we seek fitting language to borrow,
To add yet another sad link to the chain?
Sure none but an angel could bend to the strain.

And yet even he, had he gazed on the sight,
And were asked to record it in mansions of light,
Had he heard the loud wailing so painfully deep,
At the sad recollection that angel would weep.

Then how shall a mortal presume to unfold
The tale that could never by angels be told?
How breathe the sad notes of the mournful refrain?
We must pass o'er the scene of such terrible pain.

With a fervent heart-prayer that the God of all love,
May send consolation and strength from above,
With blessings that none but a God can impart,
To soothe and to comfort the poor stricken heart.

May the widow trust always His power to defend,
May she prove Him her truest, her tenderest friend;
May the fatherless little ones yield to His care,
He'll guide and protect them though father's not there.

We pray that our wounded ones, Father, may share,
Thy ministering angel's attendance and care,
That soon from their pain they may hope to be free,
And render their rescued lives back unto Thee.

We pray Thee to guard and most graciously save
Our gallant explorers, so daring and brave,
Such hearts, we are sure, must have honoured the name
Of England's proud heroes we boast of in fame.

We thank Thee, kind Father of earth and of heaven,
For aid to the suffering, so readily given;
May the blessing of those who were ready to fall,
Like a halo of glory encircle them all.

Ye wealthy, on whom the fair goddess has smiled,
Who know not the struggles of poverty's child,
In pity respond to humanity's call,
That we soon may rejoice in provision for all.

If ye give to the poor, ye but lend to the Lord,
'Tis the safest investment, He well can afford
To give good per cent. in a prosperous store,
With a kingdom of glory and life evermore.

Then give in the Name of the One we adore,
Who commended the widow, though small was her store :
Remember the cup of cold water was blest,
Then throw in your gift, ye shall fail not the rest.

Such deeds of benevolence, kindness, and love,
Though sown on this earth, shall be garnered above :
Shall shine to your honour and glory at last,
When these painful bereavements for ever are past.

IN MEMORIAM.

[Lines suggested by the Sunderland Catastrophe, by which nearly 200 Children were killed.]

Poor, innocent darlings, whose pen shall portray
The heartrending scenes of that ill-fated day ?
Whose hand but an angel's their sufferings can trace ?
Whose love but a God's meet the sorrowful case ?

Poor, heartstricken mourners, your grief must be deep,
And well may your country in sympathy weep;
Though carefully chosen, our words must be vain,
Our efforts must fail in this terrible strain.

Not yet could we ask you your tears to restrain,
For the overcharged heart must find vent for its pain;
From those silent, but eloquent, tokens of sorrow,
The grief-burdened spirit much comfort can borrow.

But, oh! while you weep for your innocent dead,
Dream not that for ever life's pleasures are fled;
Forget not that yet through this dense cloud of sorrow,
Ye shall hail the grand dawn of a glorious morrow.

This sorrow, remember, belongs but to earth,
We are all of us heirs to a nobler birth;
This wave on life's ocean, this loud-breaking swell,
Has but wafted your loved ones with angels to dwell.

Scarce closed were the bright little eyes in this death,
Scarce gone from the lov'd little frame the last breath,
Scarce fell the first tear in this wild burst of grief,
Ere the bright little spirits had found sweet relief.

Think not, weeping mothers, your little ones lay
Unnoticed by all as they thus passed away;
Dream not that no loving hand smoothed the pale brow,
Or those lips were unkissed that can tell you not now.

Oh! no, not alone did your little ones die,
Let the thought ever cheer you, God's angels were nigh,
Ever bent on some mission of mercy and love,
They bore them from earth to God's mansions above.

Reflect that your loss is your child's richest gain,
Freed once and for ever from sorrow and pain;
No sin shall e'er tempt them, no blight can destroy
Your sweet cherub girl, or your bright angel boy.

No less are they yours because gone from your sight,
No less do they love in those realms of delight,
No dream of forgetfulness ever can chase
The fond recollection of mother's sweet face.

Thus nurtured and trained in that bright summer land,
Oh! say will they not form a noble young band,
Is the prize they have gained, and the home they have found,
Not a bright cheering spot 'mid the darkness around?

Then live, mothers, live, for your little ones' home,
Where away from your side never more shall they roam;
Where the lovely young flowers ye thought faded and gone,
Ye shall find in rich beauty have ever bloomed on.

TO THE MEMORY OF LORD FREDERICK CAVENDISH.

Where the weary heart for ever
    Evermore in peace may rest—
Where the wicked enter never—
    Frederick lives, supremely blest.

THE POET'S WREATH.

Where no farewell words are spoken,
    Where no tear-drop dims the eye,
Where no loving hearts are broken,
    Frederick lives, no more to die.

Where no bold assassin meets him,
    Where no fear his heart can chill,
Where a loving mother greets him,
    Frederick there is happy still.

Where no storm clouds ever darken,
    Where no sickness taints the air,
Where to cherubs' songs he'll hearken,
    Frederick finds a home more fair.

Where the sunny skies are brightest,
    Where the flowers forget to fade,
Where once aching hearts are lightest,
    Frederick finds a welcome shade.

Where heaven's kind and holy Father,
    Smiles approval on him now,
While the angels round him gather,
    Place the crown upon his brow.

Yes, the victor's crown adorns him,
    Richly gemm'd by Christian prayer ;
England as a nation mourns him,
    Angels shout him welcome there.

There while seraph bands surround him,
    While their anthems louder swell,
Let us, 'mid the grand resounding,
    Bid our martyr'd one farewell.

LILLY MAY, OR THE BACHELOR'S STORY.

I saw her in her youthful pride,
  So beautiful and fair,
Nor dream't that aught could e'er betide,
  To cloud that brow with care.

I heard the music of her voice,
  Like evening's soothing chime,
That well-known song, "Fond heart rejoice,"
  She sang in strains sublime.

I knew her gentle winning smile
  Was sought by not a few,
And even I, though firm a while,
  At last had yielded too.

And if it be to mortals given,
  Amid life's busy whirl,
I think, as Angels love in heaven,
  I lov'd that gentle girl.

And if not wisely, far too well,
  I lov'd, yet lov'd in vain,
Would heaven that few like me might tell
  Of slighted love's deep pain!

I was not fortune's favoured child,
  And could not offer gold,
And she, alas! so good and mild,
  To one of wealth was sold.

A mother's pride had led the way,
    By prayer and tear and sigh ;
And she, accustomed to obey,
    Bade me a fond "Good bye!"

Yet once again I saw her stand,
    A fair and lovely bride ;
I saw another take the hand,
    For which I would have died,

Not caring then where'er I went,
    Or what fate had in store,
From home and friends my steps I bent,
    And sought a distant shore.

And there in time as though to shame,
    Or recompense the past,
Proud fortune smiled, and I could claim,
    A wealthy name at last.

But ah! too late! the golden tide
    For me had deign'd to flow ;
It could not now my sorrow hide,
    Or soothe my heart's deep woe.

Twelve years I wandered sad, and lone,
    Along life's cheerless way,
Hoping that time might yet atone,
    And chase my grief away.

But rest came not, it could not be,
    Too long I'd worn the chain ;
There never came the day for me,
    When I could love again.

At length, once more I trod the soil
    Of this my native land,
Where England's sons for honest toil,
    May proudly foremost stand.

I reached my childhood's home at last,
    A waiting mother wept!
But father from her side had passed,
    And in the graveyard slept.

Too late I came, his life was o'er,
    Too late I came to save;
Death, cruel death, had been before,
    And claimed him for the grave.

Why comes not death to those who pray,
    To those who wish to die?
The poet's muse declines to say,
    And echo answers "Why?"

Time passed, and I had ceased to roam,
    I could no longer stray:
My gold had cheered the dear old home,
    And brought a brighter day.

'Twas long before I breathed the name
    That yet had power to thrill;
I felt like inspiration's flame,
    A secret dread of ill.

And when at last I dared to ask
    If all with her was well,
I saw it was a bitter task,
    The mournful truth to tell.

The one I shall not call a man,
  Who lured her from my side,
Had changed, as only such men can,
  And turned life's treacherous tide

Wave after wave, in rapid whirl,
  Drew o'er her darkened life ;
And soon they knew my once fond girl,
  A sad, neglected wife.

He squandered all his wealth away,
  In reckless sin and shame,
And left the once bright Lilly May,
  With nothing but his name.

He crossed the ocean's foaming tide,
  Fresh fields of sin to find ;
She sought a home her grief to hide,
  With strangers, poor, but kind.

Her mother long before had passed
  From earthly scenes away,
And deeply mourned the pride at last,
  That led her heart astray.

And would you know, if e'er again
  In life we ever meet,
I fain would answer "Spare that pain,
  And teach me to forget?"

But no, too long I've borne the pain,
  Fond memory lingers yet ;
Too long, I've loved, though lov'd in vain,
  This heart can ne'er forget.

We met, but ah ! it was the last,
  And fraught with bitter pain ;
That sorrow's hour of withering blast
  I could not live again.

One lovely night, with feelings strange,
  I wandered out to stroll,
For thoughts of some impending change
  Disturbed my weary soul.

I lingered near the church-yard scene,
  And thought of those who slept :
To father's grave I'd often been,
  And o'er those ashes wept.

Again I sought that sacred spot,
  To ease my throbbing breast :
And wondered if the dead forgot
  Those who still sigh for rest.

I there in sad and pensive state
  Reviewed life's dreary way,
And wondered why such bitter fate
  For me and Lilly May.

I rose at last, o'ercome with care,
  And turned with noiseless tread,
When on my ear a murmured prayer
  Seem'd echoed from the dead !

I could not then have told you why
  That murmur thrill'd me through,
'Twas but a feebly uttered cry,
  "Oh ! Father, take me too."

But something in the voice awoke
    Deep echoes of the past,
And had I not kind Heaven invoked,
    That hour had been my last.

For reason trembled on her throne,
    And life seem'd ebbing fast,
But darkest hours sometimes atone,
    And blessings prove at last.

"Twas thus with me, the crisis o'er,
    There dawn'd a clearer light :
I vow'd, whatever lay before,
    To live and do the right

Strong in this new resolve I turned
    In search of her who prayed ;
The moon in brilliant beauty burned,
    As o'er the dead I strayed.

Soon by her friendly light I saw
    A form I knew too well ;
I stood transfixed in silent awe,
    With feelings none may tell.

There by a little well trimmed grave,
    Which spoke of much fond care,
Knelt her I would have died to save,
    Weeping in wild despair.

An aged female lingering near,
    Most gently raised her head :
Again she murmur'd " Leave me here !
    I'll stay with little Fred."

Quick as the lightning's swiftest gleam,
    I hastened to her side,
Forgetting all life's weary dream,
    And years of sorrow's tide.

Gently, her wasted hand I took,
    And whispered "Come with me!"
She started, gave one long fond look,
    And murmured "Yes, 'tis he!"

The old familiar happy smile
    I knew in youth's bright day,
Played o'er her lovely face awhile,
    Then slowly passed away.

And in its stead a look of pain,
    Those marble features swept;
Oh! in that hour of nature's strain,
    An angel might have wept.

But words must fail, none e'er can know
    All that I suffered then,
I could not write that scene of woe,
    'Twould task an angel's pen.

I passed that long, sad, dreary night,
    With friends around her bed,
And knew when dawned the early light
    That Lilly May was dead.

She spoke but once, we saw, with pain,
    That life was ebbing fast,
And whispered "We shall meet again!"
    Then sank in peace at last.

We laid her with her little Fred,
    Where long she'd pray'd to be,
And though they speak of her as dead,
    She is not dead to me.

I know that on a brighter shore,
    Where beams eternal day,
Where pride or death shall part no more,
    I'll meet dear Lilly May.

HOMELESS.

The old man turn'd at his cottage door,
    And wept a fond farewell,
As scenes from happier days of yore
    Came o'er him like a spell.
Since first he brought his fair young bride,
    Just fifty years had passed;
'Twas there she lived, 'twas there she died,
    Her only home and last.

There, through this weary world of strife,
    They'd borne, with many a sorrow;
And there the sunnier shades of life
    Had brightened many a morrow.
There, too, had blossom'd one by one,
    A family of seven,
Who since had gather'd one by one
    'Neath fairer skies in heaven.

And yesterday had borne away
    His wife, so tried and true;
Well might he weep, well might he pray,
    That he might die there too.
Too feeble now to work for bread,
    His last-earn'd shilling spent:
The workhouse but remain'd instead,
    And thither he was bent.

Slowly he raised his drooping head,
    And gave one last sad look,
And then with feeble, faltering tread,
    His weary way he took.
Yet once again he paused: 'twas when
    He reach'd the churchyard gate;
One fond good-bye to them, and then
    He'd welcome cruel fate.

They saw him slowly wend his way
    Across the sacred ground,
And there when pass'd the light of day,
    The poor old man was found.
The summer's gentle breezes play'd
    Around his snow-white head,
Oh! not in vain that soul had pray'd,
    The homeless one was dead.

And there they laid him down to rest,
    With all he'd lov'd on earth,
And now with them for ever blest
    He finds a nobler birth;
While they who might have found him bread,
    And cheer'd his latest hours,
Now raise a monument instead,
    And deck his grave with flowers.

Oh! when will these things cease to be,
    When shall we learn to know,
The heart's rich tribute, pure and free,
    Is not in flimsy show?
When shall we to the living prove
    As sister, or as brother?
The truest hearts are those that move
    In kindness to another.

A SATIRE.

    Whether I please or whether I tease,
        I'll give you my own honest mind,
    If the cap should fit you may wear it a bit,
        If not, you may leave it behind. —*John Ploughman.*

What has he done? Are you really quite sane
    That you ask with such scorn and contempt!
I certainly thought your most excellent brain
    From freaks of such nature exempt.

I credited you with a little more sense,
    A little more charity, too,
Than to rail at a name with such sorry pretence
    Because it belongs to a Blue.

You have liv'd in our midst ever bent on your gain,
    Full forty long years if all told,
And now you are asking, with righteous disdain,
    What others have done with their gold.

And well may you ask, if by asking you mean
    To remind me you've done quite as well;
But keep yourself cool, it can easily be seen,
    For the past will most faithfully tell.

Just put to one side all this anger, I pray,
    Let reason, not passion, control;
I heard you one Sunday decidedly say
    That anger would ruin the soul.

You spoke to the young of the beautiful life,
    Of the lowly, despised Nazarene,
And warn'd them to cease from dissension and strife,
    Which a curse to their country had been.

I think, too, you said that you loved to look back
    On your life's busy wonderful day.
'Twas pleasant to roam o'er the old beaten track,
    And see what you'd done by the way.

Then wander with me through that mystical shade,
    That has yielded such pleasure to you,
Perhaps a few scenes of a different grade
    I may find in a careful review.

You must wake up your memory, else I shall fail,
    Without her most wonderful light;
Put passion to sleep and let reason prevail,
    Give conscience her place for to-night.

Go back over years that have passed like a dream,
    O'er bright sunny hours that are fled;
Still backward, Oh! memory, bear on thy stream,
    Till we stand with the beautiful dead.

Yes, there is the scene I have sought to unveil,
  There one of the laurels you've won,
Now tell me if pleasant reflections prevail
  As you gaze on the form of your son?

A prodigal truly, but driven from home
  By stern hypocritical sway,
Compelled a poor desolate outcast to roam
  Till he fall on life's pitiless way.

Strange hands close the eyes that once smiled in your own,
  Strange lips kiss the cold marble brow,
Had your own selfish heart the same tenderness shown,
  That son might have honoured you now.

Another scene rises, a poor widow's child
  Lies tossing in fever and pain,
And the poor mother, almost distracted and wild,
  Appeals to your conscience in vain.

Her rent is quite due, but her boy must be fed,
  Or soon he'll be under the sod,
But you sternly demand what would furnish him bread,
  Then tell her to trust in her God.

Yet another scene comes from the shades of the past
  Where you rob a poor man of his place;
And the dark dreary sorrows that round him were cast,
  Yet tell to your shame and disgrace.

He pleads with a pitying sense of despair
  That justice from you may be given,
You coolly refuse, but presumptiously dare
  To hope for the mercy of heaven.

One more, 'tis the home of your true-hearted brother
    Now shatter'd in spirits and health,
Too noble to live by oppressing another,
    He owns neither title nor wealth.

In happier years he had saved your poor life,
    By a terrible risk of his own,
And now after years of stern poverty's strife,
    To you he is almost unknown.

Thank God, he yet lives and the power is with you
    To save from a heavier sorrow ;
His health and his prospects in kindness renew,
    And brighten his future to-morrow.

Talk less about Jesus and practice His life,
    Seek not for a false gilded fame,
Cheer poverty's pathway and lessen its strife,
    And then you will honour His name.

Go comfort the widow and fatherless child,
    Go dry the poor sufferer's tear,
Go save a lov'd son from the world's dreary wild,
    And a mother's fond breaking heart cheer.

Do this, and the future shall blot out the past,
    And thy spirit with joy shall yet see
That the beautiful deeds in this life thou hads't cast
    Have borne a rich harvest for thee.

SONG—THE WANDERING BOY.

Wearily, drearily, lonely and sad,
  I have wandered the long, cheerless day;
One smile would have made me feel hopeful and glad,
  And brightened my life's darkened way.
But none seemed to pity me, none seemed to care,
  All pass'd me contemptuously by;
Would God I could breathe a poor sinner's last prayer,
  Then calmly and peacefully die.

CHORUS.
Oh, would that my mother were with me to-night,
  No hunger or cold should I fear,
Her love would make life again peaceful and bright,
  Oh, would that my mother were here.

Oh, why did I leave her? What demon could tempt?
  What power impelled me to roam?
If the ills which have followed my soul could have dreamt,
  I had never thus wandered from home.
I cannot forget how my poor mother wept,
  As I tore from her loving embrace,
Though storms of deep darkness my pathway have swept,
  That scene they could never efface.
        CHORUS—Oh, would that, &c.

This Bible she gave me, is all I have left,
  She whispered, "You'll read it, I know;
And when of all comfort thy soul is bereft,
  Remember, I pray for thee, Joe."
Oh, surely, those prayers have not been in vain,
  And, perhaps, all this sorrow were best;
If I only could reach the old home once again,
  I should prize such an haven of rest.
        CHORUS—Oh, would that, &c.

Some shelter I'll find from the cold bitter blast,
    And wait for the dawning of day;
And surely, some heart will feel pity at last,
    And grant me some help by the way.
Already this darkness seems passing away,
    Already I feel a new joy;
Heaven spare my dear mother to welcome the day
    Which brings back her wandering boy.
              Chorus—Oh, would that, &c.

SONG.—THE WANDERING BOY'S RETURN.

Again the loved shores of my dear native land
    Resound to my now joyous tread;
And visions that greet me on every hand,
    Seem gifted with life from the dead.
'Tis well that the darkness befriends my return
    To the scene of my earliest years,
For ill could I brook that a stranger should spurn,
    'Twould awake but my bitterest tears.

        Oh! England, my fatherland,
            Home of the free;
        Back from a stranger land,
            Welcome to thee.

Not many will know me, how changed I must seem;
    How meanly and poorly I'm clad;
But the mother of many a beautiful dream,
    Will know her poor wandering lad.

Oh, yes, she will know and will love none the less,
    But call me her darling once more ;
And I, if but spared, will her future life bless,
    And her long weeping days shall be o'er.
                          Oh ! England, &c.

How calm is the night, what a sense of repose,
    E'en the moon seems a holier light ;
And a rapturous joy my poor heart overflows,
    For my boyhood's loved home is in sight.
Yes, there is my home, just the same as of old,
    The home of my earliest prayer ;
And dearer than all the world's treasures of gold,
    Is the peace that awaiteth me there.
                          Oh ! England, &c.

Softly, and almost with reverent tread,
    I enter the low narrow gate ;
One moment and all the past seasons of dread
    Will be lost in a happier fate.
But listen 'tis surely no freak of the brain
    For I hear a soft murmuring prayer,
'Tis the voice I have longed but to hear once again,
    I will enter and kneel with her there.
                          Oh ! England, &c.

A CHRISTMAS EVE'S VISION.

'Twas Christmas Eve, I had wandered alone
    To a quiet and beautiful spot,
Where many brief hours of repose I had known,
    As the cares of the world were forgot.

The time, and the place, with the silence around,
    Woke memories joyous and sad ;
One moment a feeling of sorrow profound,
    The next I was wondrously glad.

For wave after wave, at fond memory's bid,
    Rolled back o'er the sands of old time :
Revealing lost treasures, long buried and hid,
    With a faithfulness truly sublime.

Scenes varied as life's ever varying sky,
    Swept past on that hurrying stream :
And familiar echoes there floated me by--
    Like a far away beautiful dream.

On sped the mysterious current, until
    All the present seemed merged in the past,
Till every vestige of life's bitter ill
    Had pass'd from my spirit at last.

Then a lull and a calm, and a conscious repose,
    With a joy that was born not of earth ;
Till I thought I had left this cold region of woes,
    And pass'd to a happier birth.

No longer alone ; many forms that I knew,
    Who had gone from this life's weary care,
Who had been to their God ever faithful and true,
    Most joyously welcom'd me there.

A strain of soft melody, borne on the breeze,
    Seem'd to breathe of a yet fairer land :
And softly I murmur'd, "Sure, strains such as these,
    Must belong to some holier band !"

"Most truly, my friend," whispered one who was near,
   "They are those of superior birth :
But the words are familiar, couldst thou but hear,
   For their song is an echo from earth."

"But come, thou shalt see," and he led me away,
   Past scenes most entrancingly fair :
Till I found, with a feeling of grief and dismay,
   I was nearing this cold world of care.

Still swept on the beautiful cadence ; as yet
   Still around me were beings most bright,
And the cold dreary chill of earth's darkness had set
   In a flood of celestial light.

By some wonderful power I could see at a glance,
   Many thousands of earth's weary throng ;
Some keeping the night with a feast and a dance,
   And some with the drink and a song.

The beautiful maiden—some fond mother's pride,
   And joy of her life here below ;
"Would God," I exclaimed, "thou hadst happily died,
   Ere thy beauty had fallen so low."

Many manly young forms, I had thought would adorn
   An Englishman's long-honoured name :
Of manhood's true glory and dignity shorn
   I beheld, in those regions of shame.

As I gazed on the scene with a feeling of pain,
   And a sigh for such wreck of life's treasure,
I listened in vain for the beautiful strain
   That had yielded my soul such a pleasure.

But the being who led me, in sadness explained
    This unholy and sin-loving throng :
Their souls not attuned, nor their hearts ever trained,
    Had no part in that beautiful song.

But another scene rose, of a beauty most rare,
    Of a higher and nobler blend ;—
Would heaven such proofs of Samaritan's care
    To the ends of the world might extend.

A few noble souls, whose delight is to bless
    And rescue earth's perishing poor ;
Whose giving makes not their abundance seem less,
    But eternity's treasures more sure.

From the garrets and cellars and streets of our land,
    From the depths of much folly and sin—
A sadly neglected and desolate band—
    Those angels have gathered them in.

In their beautiful homes, so amazingly bright,
    They have spread them a plenteous repast ;
Till they dream they have left the cold earth's dreary night,
    And entered God's heaven at last.

Fairy forms move amongst them, like beings of light,
    To their untutor'd natures they seem,
And beauties unnumbered bewilder their sight—
    Enhancing the beautiful dream.

Skill'd fingers sweep softly the musical keys :
    Trained voices re-echo the song ;
Till a mystical wave of celestial breeze,
    Breaks over that mystified throng.

THE POET'S WREATH.

Chords silent for years, are awaken'd at last,
    By the touch of true sympathy's wand ;
And the veil that had shrouded life's beautiful past,
    Is withdrawn by some fair Angel's hand.

Scenes dear to the heart of some wanderer there,
    Rise clear and distinct on the tide ;
With the words of a dear and fond mother's last prayer,
    And her blessing, as calmly she died.

Then slowly arose a tall form in that crowd,
    'Twas that fond mother's noble-brow'd son ;
Who spoke with deep sorrow and head meekly bow'd,
    Of the sinful career he had run.

But the sympathy shown and the songs he had heard,
    Woke memories painful, yet sweet :
And the deepest recess of his nature was stirr'd,
    So to live he that mother might meet.

From every heart rose a tribute of praise,
    Which resounded throughout the vast throng,
And the beings around me, of heavenly grace,
    Took up the glad strains of the song.

And again rose the melody, wondrously clear,
    Which at first so bewildered my soul ;
Now richer, and sweeter, through heaven's high sphere
    The beautiful symphonies roll.

And the hearts of the few, who so faithful and true,
    Struck the chord of that glorious strain,
From Him to whom all the world's homage is due,
    Hear a whisper, "Your work is not vain.

Ye are bless'd indeed, who delight to obey;
  Whose fruits of devotion I see;
In all ye have done unto these by the way,
  Ye have done even more unto Me."

Oh, ye who can waken such chords by the way,
  And brighten such lives' dreary morn,
Remember their blessing shall cheer on life's way,
  And your crown of rejoicing adorn.

But beyond, and above, and exceeding all this,
  What joy when this earth-life is run,
To behold in the homes of celestial bliss,
  Many such, whom to God ye have won.

AN IMPROMPTU FAREWELL.

These farewells will soon be over,
  All these sorrows soon be past.
We shall then at last discover
  Purer friendship that shall last.

Here we part, and know not whether
  Time permits again to meet,
But the fond hearts there together
  Find their happiness complete.

Here the waters may divide us,
  Dearest ties some chance may sever,
Never there such fates betide us
  Farewell words are hushed for ever.

Here our peaceful homes are entered,
    Borne away our fairest flowers,
There we find 'mid pleasures centred,
    All we mourned in grief's dark hours.

Not for ever, not for ever,
    Shall these tears bedim our eyes,
Death or parting ne'er can sever,
    Once we meet beyond the skies.

Brighter homes are there awaiting,
    Fairer scenes and healthier clime,
Through eternal ages dating
    Far beyond the reach of time.

There the soul progresseth ever,
    While those ceaseless ages roll
Onward ever, backward never,
    Is the motto of the soul.

Then let farewell words be spoken,
    Linger not o'er pathways trod ;
Hearts may yet, though sad and broken,
    Find sweet rest, —then trust your God.

WOMAN'S MISSION.

When the earth in her beauty stood forth at the call
Of nature's great Architect Founder of all,
When angels admiringly gaz'd on the scene,
How gloriously fair the young world must have been.

How the sun in his newly-lit splendour would gleam
On the flower-bedeck'd earth and the smooth gliding stream,
While the feather'd young choristers, loudly and long,
Must have thrilled the whole earth as they sang their first
    song.

Around and above, all was wondrously fair,
No dark looming shadow, no tempest was there ;
One exquisite grandeur from cloudlet to sod,
Proclaim'd the undoubted existence of God.

But fairer than all must have been the retreat,
Where man, the first man, in his glory we meet ;
Sole heir to the world, indisputably his,
And yet, even yet, incomplete was his bliss.

Alone, the young Adam might oft have been found
In some favourite seat, gazing pensively round ;
While fancy would picture, as fancy will dare,
A scene more entrancing, a vision more fair.

And musing enwrapt, how his soul must have thrill'd,
As he fancied the void in his lonely heart fill'd :
For he knew his indulgent Creator would not
Leave a want unsupplied, or a blessing forgot.

Thus calmly and peacefully resting on this,
He quietly slumbers, nor dreams of his bliss,
Till waking, refresh'd he discovers with pride,
He's no longer alone, but is blest with a bride.

Presented by heaven's great Author of good,
Before him resplendent in beauty she stood,
While He who had form'd her so perfect and free,
His comfort and helpmeet design'd her to be.

This, then, is your mission, ye daughters of earth,
Seek well to fulfil it, disgrace not your birth ;
Oh ! fritter not idly the power that is given,
Ye may drive to perdition, or raise them to heaven.

Plead not that our mother Eve fail'd in her trust,
Though painful the thought, let her daughters be just,
That one sin reduced her in sorrow to roam,
And robb'd her of Eden, her beautiful home.

Then think of her kindly, no doubt from that hour
She wisely exerted her womanly power ;
Her life must have prov'd not in vain was she given,
If she robb'd him of earth, she restored him to heaven.

And sure 'tis a glorious mission of bliss,
To brighten his path through a world such as this ;
To aid him when wearied of earth and its cares,
Restore him with hope, and restrain him with prayers.

To bear with his weaknesses, follies and sin,
And patiently try from those follies to win ;
To render his home what at first it was meant,
His haven of rest, his throne of content.

Oh ! woman, remember your God-given trust,
Be patient and tender, be faithful and just ;
Be all that is lovely, and prove, while you can,
God's noblest and best is the helpmeet to man.

TO THE MEMORY OF MRS. LANG BRIDGE.

[My friend of early years, whose beautiful and blameless life throws one more ray of light across the shadow'd path of mortal strife, and whose lov'd and honour'd memory adds one more link to the mysterious chain of love which ever seeks to draw the aspiring soul onward and heavenward.]

Some lives in their day,
Over earth's dreary way,
Like stars the wild night shades adorning,
Seem heralds of light,
Ever radiant and bright
From the rays of celestial morning.

Of such was the one
Who her earth-course has run,
But whose memory never shall perish :
Hearts many and true,
That her excellence knew,
Many fond recollections will cherish.

No clarion tongue
Sang her praises among
Those whom the world hasteth to honour,
But we who can tell
She hath lived her life well
Know that heaven's own signet is on her.

All the graces that blend,
And unitedly lend
A charm to their humble possessor,
Mark'd her beautiful life,
As a maiden or wife,
And long shall our grateful hearts bless her.

In the archives of heaven
Her name is engraven
In undying splendour and beauty ;
And ever shall tell
How most faithfully well
She acquitted herself of her duty.

And though she has pass'd
From the earth-side at last
To her 'tis a glorious transition ;
For the work of her love
Will develop above,
To a higher and holier mission.

And they are still blest,
Who so long have possess'd,
Such a gem in their household adorning :
Would they follow her light,
She would lead through earth's night
To heaven's own beautiful morning.

Dear friend of my youth,
May the Father of Truth
Ever grant it my earnest ambition,
To live out earth's day
In the same noble way,
Till I make the same glorious transition.

MAN'S INHUMANITY TO MAN.

I knew him in life ere a sorrow had cast
    Its shade over earth's sunny sky ;
Ere sickness had bound him, or death's cruel blast,
    Had warned him that he, too, must die.

His beautiful home every comfort could boast
    This world's sordid wealth can obtain ;
And they who could flatter and honour him most,
    Sometimes his cold favour might gain.

A sacred position of honour and trust,
    In proof of religion, he held ;
And woe to the poor erring creature of dust
    Whom he fancied had slightly rebelled.

No mercy, no pity, no thought, would he show ;
    No tale of distress would he hear ;
He was proud and self-righteous, and gloried to know
    He had never been moved by a tear.

With a few he could pass as a great and good man,
    For they measured his heart by his gold ;
But the poor honest toilers, the hard working clan,
    Could his real secret nature unfold.

They could tell you of hearts that had languished and bled;
    Of noble souls plunged in deep sorrow ;
Because he withheld what would furnish them bread,
    And brighten their darkened to-morrow.

They could tell you of those who had prayed him to save,
  From a life of starvation and dread;
Who, in accents more touching than words from the grave,
  Had pleaded for work and for bread.

But, no! this inhuman professor indeed
  Had never been known to relent;
They were told he had nothing to do with their need,
  And empty away had been sent.

My poor brother Burns! I would cry thus with thee:
  Oh, why such contemptible scorn?
Oh, why should such cold cruel tyrants as he
  Compel us to suffer and mourn?

But dying-time came, and he left his proud name
  With his titled estates all behind him;
And a beautiful monument, reared to his fame,
  Will show, if you wish, where to find him.

The minister prayed—as all ministers do—
  That the life of our friend might be blest;
And urged us to live out our lives quite as true,
  And earn the same glorious rest.

Now, I having doubts, as to whether or no,
  This man of profession and creeds
To the brightest and best of all heavens should go
  To sing of his noble earth deeds:—

And knowing a way to that wonderful land—
  Though a private one only, 'tis true—
Yet this I would have you at once understand,
  It leads to the grand final view.

The key is in nature's own keeping, I know,
    And sometimes I wait for her long ;
But yet I can tempt her her secrets to show
    If I breathe her a poet's sweet song :

Availing myself of this wonderful tide
    I launched from the shores of old time,
And soon I was far from these regions of pride
    And filled with a rapture sublime.

Away, still away, over worlds fair and bright,
    Still higher I soared on my way ;
I left far behind me the shadows of night,
    And found a more glorious day.

I entered a world of most exquisite bliss —
    A region of holier birth,
Outvieing a thousand fair worlds such as this, —
    Eclipsing thy grandeur, oh earth.

I gazed on its cloudless and beautiful sky,
    Illum'd by celestial light ;
While sweet little choristers flitted me by,
    Of plumage transcendently bright.

Its rivers like rippling silver and gold
    In musical waves swept along ;
While thousands of wondrous delights, never told,
    Enlivened its murmuring song.

Trees fairer than any this earth ever knew,
    And laden with fruits of the clime ;
And flowerets still fairer than Eden e'er grew,
    All bow'd to the wonderful chime.

And sounding afar, and yet near, came the swell
    Of voices so happy and free ;
So wondrously sweet I was puzzled to tell
    Whether angels or mortals they'd be.

I turned my bewildering gaze all around,
    In search of some angel, or friend ;
But met only grandeur more vast and profound,
    Which seemed of an infinite end.

Transfixed by some wonderful mystical spell ;
    O'ercome by a sense of such bliss,
I murmured, "Oh, is there no being to tell
    Who dwells in a world such as this?"

My murmur was heard, for before me one stood
    In a halo of beauty sublime,
Whose life on the earth had been wondrously good,
    Ere he passed from the regions of time.

He was known in our midst as the working man's friend,
    Many sorrows to him have been told,
And to all would his practical pity extend,
    For he worshipped no idol of gold.

He was full of that mercy which comes from above,
    He would bend to a brother in need,
He could win a fond heart by his pitying love,
    He was Benjamin truly indeed.

He liv'd out this life unassuming and free,
    Nor cared for the world's bitter scorn,
Would heaven that many more gems such as he
    This life's darkened skies might adorn.

He smiled as of old while he kindly replied,
　"To thy murmur I gladly respond;
They dwell o'er that silvery, rippling tide,
　Who have earned its bright glories beyond."

"By their life on the earth, by their mission of love,
　By the help on the way they have given;
By the honour they brought to the Father above,
　They have entered those regions of heaven."

"Not by the distinction of name on the earth,
　Nor the weight of their silver and gold,
Have they gained their position of holier birth,
　But by deeds that have never been told."

"Not because they have given their wealth to adorn
　Some proud architectural plan,
But because they have brightened some life's dreary morn,
　And rescued some poor fellow-man."

"Not those who have crushed the poor hard toiling slave,
　Till he pine for a rest 'neath the sod;
Not those who gain wealth through oppression's dark wave,
　Can enter these realms of our God."

"See there," and the bright one directed my sight
　To a fleecy-like cloud by the way,
Which slowly, but surely, grew clearer and bright,
　Then passed like a beam from the day.

Disclosing a scene of most exquisite joy,
　Of holy and rapturous bliss;
Oh! earth, thy enchantments are surely a toy,
　Compared to the glories of this.

The lovely inhabitants, blooming and fair,
    Seemed gems of ethereal light,
No brow bore a shadow of sorrow or care,
    But glistened transcendently bright.

Their beautiful homes were a marvel to see,
    Though built not of silver or gold,
Each wonderful structure seemed clearly to me
    The page of their life to unfold.

Their work of great love on the earth they had left,
    The kind little deeds they had done,
From the child they had sheltered whom death had bereft,
    To the hearts they had lovingly won.

The thousand and one little seeds they had sown,
    The joy and the sympathy given,
With the smile of the Father, around them had grown,
    And built them this beautiful heaven.

"And now," said my guide, for by this you must know
    He had somehow detected my thought,
"To the regions still higher you could not well go,
    And he is not here whom you sought."

"From your mind I perceive he has built on the sand,
    And trusted in dogmas and creed,
Believe me, my friend, that such lives cannot stand,
    They are shallow pretences indeed."

"When such leave the earth, they awake but to find
    They have passed through its school but in vain ;
That all they have trusted is left far behind,
    And life must be worked out again."

"The one whom you seek is not far from the earth,
    For he trained not his spirit to rise,
And ere he can hope for a holier birth,
    He must work for the coveted prize."

"Thank God, he can rise from his fallen estate
    To a brighter and happier land,
For the wisdom of heaven decrees no such fate
    For the work of His own noble hand."

"Return to your world, but remember to teach
    It is life on the earth that shall tell
The crown of success, or the failure of each,
    And warn them to weave it out well."

He turned with me kindly towards this cold sphere,
    And waved a most tender adieu,
And a sweet farewell song lingers yet in my ear,
    As the happy scene fades from my view.

To me here's a lesson I tremble to learn,
    Though rendered so plain to my view,
If a home in those regions of bliss I would earn,
    My life must be holy and true.

Not yet dare I claim the Christian's fair name,
    Nor boast that to me it was given,
Not yet dare I trust to these laurels of fame,
    To win me a passport to heaven.

But, oh! I dare trust the kind Father above,
    To bless but my little earth grain,
And hope, yes I hope, through His goodness and love,
    A suitable harvest to gain.

BITTER MEMORIES: OR, THE BALLET GIRL'S REMORSE.

Oh! Memory, why bring back to-night
    The happy scenes of early years?
Why reproduce my youth's sad blight?
    Why wake again these bitter tears?

Why bring back faces far away,
    And forms I buried long ago?
Why bid the lovely vision stay?
    Why give thy waves this backward flow?

Is it because some guiding hand,
    By rays of inspiration given,
Would point me to a better land,
    And teach my weary soul of Heaven?

Or can it be, as some would say,
    That from their bright and blest abode
Some lov'd ones yet can wing their way,
    To save us from destruction's road?

Oh! could I hear but once again
    A mother's sweet forgiving voice,
'Twould calm this fever in my brain,
    And make this aching heart rejoice.

But no, I dare not hope for this,
    For well I know mine was the part
That dashed her hopes of earthly bliss,
    And broke her gentle loving heart.

Poor widow'd mother, how she wept,
    Those bitter tears I still can see,
As from the room I proudly swept
    And vow'd a ballet girl I'd be.

And well do I remember yet,
    My only brother's manly grief:
Oh! Memory, could'st thou not forget,
    And give this tortured heart relief.

Forget! Ah, never! waves roll on,
    And visions throng my restless brain,
Till every hope of life seems gone,
    And tears and prayers are all in vain.

Again I see that noble youth
    Who won my once pure girlish heart,
And as I meet his eyes of truth
    I feel how cruel 'twas to part.

The words he spoke when last we met,
    This breaking heart would fail to tell,
And as the sun in splendour set
    We spoke our final sad farewell.

And on a cold and foreign shore
    He wandered long in search of rest,
But now his toils and cares are o'er;
    In Heaven my slighted one is blest.

Yes, he is gone, and ere he died,
    His trembling fingers wrote to say:
Though parted long, and severed wide,
    For me he'd never ceased to pray.

His only hope, his one last care,
    Was that some future day might bring
The darling of his fondest prayer
    Beneath a God's protecting wing.

This little ring that once was mine,
    That could such happy scenes unfold,
He asked that once again might shine
    Upon the hand he lov'd to hold.

Enclosed within his letter came
    The little shining gem of gold,
Too well I know 'tis just the same
    As when I gave it back so cold.

And as I gaze upon it now,
    'Mid blinding tears and vain regret.
I feel across my fevered brow,
    Those loving fingers even yet.

Thy dying wish, dear sainted one,
    Shall sacred prove to me at last,
All false allurements now are gone,
    For me all sinful joys are past.

I'll wear again thy little ring
    In memory of thy constant love,
And live the life that yet shall bring
    Reunion in those realms above.

A POEM.

Dedicated to the Rev. Thomas Waugh.

"Go ye forth into all the world and preach the Gospel to every creature."

Onward, brave soldier, thy Master commands,
Go preach the glad tidings to earth's darken'd lands,
Undaunted and fearless respond to the call,
Go tell the world's millions there's mercy for all.

Go forth in the Name that hath ever prevail'd,
Go trust in the strength that hath never yet fail'd,
Pause not, though oft weary, be strong in His might,
Who has brought thee in mercy from darkness to light.

In the darkest, the vilest recesses of sin,
There are brothers and sisters, oh, gather them in;
Point the hopeless and erring ones sunk in despair,
To the God who despis'd not the publican's prayer.

Oh, teach not the poor oppress'd child of the sod,
Of a dark yawning hell and a terrible God;
But a father of tenderest pitying love,
And a possible home with the angels above.

There are God-given intellects, jewels most rare,
There are talents that angels might wish but to share,
There are souls that would shine with a lustre most bright,
Could they wake from the slumber of sin's dreary night.

Be it thine to arouse them with tenderest care,
Go win them to God by example and prayer:
Go plead that the talents so graciously lent
Henceforth to His honour and glory be spent.

Go tell the poor heart-broken mourners in sorrow,
The tears of to-day shall be gems of to-morrow ;
The stream of affection proud death cannot sever,
Its rippling wavelets roll onward for ever.

Go comfort the poor oppress'd toiler and slave,
Who longs for the quiet and rest of the grave,
Whose pleadings for justice in scorn have been pass'd,
Go tell him his God will deal justly at last.

Go warn the oppressor, though great he may be,
Go tell him of One who is mightier than he,
Who hath made of one blood all the children of men ;
And ask could he meet Him unblushingly then.

Oh, thine is a glorious mission indeed,
And for many such workers the world hath great need ;
The harvest is waiting, enough and to spare,
But where are the workers ? say, echo, oh where !

May be there are many, too many I fear,
Who are handsomely paid by some hundreds a year,
For reading a sermon or trying to speak,
And resting their brains all the rest of the week.

Toil on, noble soldier, thy labour shall tell,
When death shall demand of thy soul " Is it well ?"
When the conflict is ended and victory won,
Heaven's vault shall resound, "Well and faithfully done."

A MODERN DANIEL.

[IMPROMPTU AFTER HEARING THE REV. R. CATTERALL.]

Onward, brave Daniel, true scion of Heaven,
Glorious the work that to thee has been given ;
Work that shall tell when life's changes are past,
And the harvest of souls has been gather'd at last.

'Tis thine, 'mid the chaos and gloom of the day,
To cheer the sin-wearied ones over life's way :
From the darkest and dreariest regions of sin,
Thy mission of love must undoubtedly win.

'Tis thine to unlock the seal'd fountain of tears,
And water the grave of some life's wasted years ;
'Tis thine, when the hopeless one yields to despair,
To whisper of solace and comfort in prayer.

'Tis thine, when the waves of affliction roll nigh,
And clouds of wild fury sweep over life's sky ;
When the heart, oh! so weary, would rest 'neath the sod,
Even then thou canst prove but a merciful God.

When the cold, cruel grave hides the dearest and best,
And the breaking heart longs for the same quiet rest :
'Tis thine to uplift the dark curtain of time,
And show us them still in a happier clime.

To arouse from its slumbers the guilt-stricken soul,
To arrest the mad torrent of sin's fearful roll ;
To make the bleak wilderness blossom for heaven,
Is the grand noble work which thy Father hath given.

Then on, though the terrors of darkness assail,
Their forces combined cannot o'er thee prevail;
A convoy of angels thy footsteps attend,
And the God of all worlds is thy Guardian and Friend.

Then on, though the battle rage fiercely and long,
Still on, though thy foes may wax valiant and strong;
Ever on, till heaven's laurels are laid at thy feet,
And the angels have crowned thee a victor complete.

HONOUR TO CHRIST.

"Woe unto you rich for ye have your consolation."—Words of Jesus.

Oh! had this good Jesus but lived in our day,
'Mid the strife and contention of tyranny's sway,
Did He know but the struggles of poverty's child,
Would He warn the oppressors in language so mild?

Would He visit the wealthy in comfort and ease,
Surrounded by all that could dazzle and please?
Would He list to their mean and self-righteous protest,
That they honoured His Name and were seeking His rest?

Would He join in their worship and hark to their prayers,
While they thanked the kind Father that heaven was theirs;
That of all He had given them, all He had lent,
They had rendered Him back a most honest per cent.?

Would He gaze on their beautiful mansions so grand,
And count up the cost of their well-chosen land?
Would He measure their love by the strength of their gold,
And assign them a kingdom of riches untold?

Oh, no! He would gather around Him the mass,
Of the poor oppressed toilers, the hard working class,
Whose pleadings for justice unheeded have passed,
To the Great Arbitrator of Heaven at last.

And gazing around Him in pitying love,
At a sight which has moved e'en the angels above,
While His tender heart swelled with affection and pain,
Those words from His lips would re-echo again.

And pointing to those who would labour for bread,
Compelled to accept a mere pittance instead,
He would ask if an honour to Him it was meant,
All this terrible strife and this bitter lament.

He would ask if His teachings were followed by those
Who might have prevented such heartrending woes;
Had they lov'd but their Maker instead of their gold,
These tales of privation had never been told.

No doubt they would answer as many before
Have answered, " Dear Jesus, Thy name we adore ;
We give of our substance Thy cause to uphold,
These walls to Thy honour were built with our gold.

"We enter Thy temple each Sabbath to pray ;
We warn wicked sinners that come in our way ;
We thought we had served Thee most faithful and true,
And hoped the 'Well done !' had been justly our due."

We think we can see, as with righteous disdain,
He points to the poor oppressed workers again,
And replies with a sadness most touching to see :
"Had ye done it to these, ye had done it to Me.

" 'Tis not the cold glitter of tinsel and dust,
That sometime must pass to oblivion's rust,
Nor yet the proud meaningless forms that I see,
These cannot, and will not, bring glory to Me.

" 'Tis not in the gift of your gold I delight,
More precious by far is the poor widow's mite :
'Tis the soul's true affection unfettered and free,
Alone can bring glory and honour to Me.

"My Father's grand temple fills earth, air, and skies,
And nature's rich tributes incessantly rise,
While angels re-echo the strains as they roll,
Through the beautiful realms of the glorified soul.

"Yet here among men I had thought to be true,
From whom I had hoped a rich harvest was due,
I find only discord, contention, and strife,
For the gold that shall fade with this uncertain life.

"Look round on the homes of your toilers and see
What painful distress in some cases there be,
And ask if it answers the Name ye profess,
And if truth be your motto, that truth ye'll confess.

"These poor honest workers would willingly toil
For that which My Father sends free to your soil ;
So free that for all there is much and to spare ;
Then honour your God by accepting their prayer.

"Let work but be given and labour be paid ;
Let honesty's stamp be the mark of your trade ;
Let justice and mercy triumphantly reign,
And peace and contentment shall bless you again.

"Oh ! list to their pleadings, and do what is right,
And chase from your country this dark weary night ;
Do this, and ere long your lov'd England shall see,
Ye have honoured your nation and glorified Me.

"And ye, honest toilers, I here would implore,
Bear patiently on till the conflict is o'er ;
Let peace like a halo, encircle your fame,
And the world shall confess ye have honoured My Name."

SPIRIT LOVE.

The day had been one of June's brightest and best,
And the sun's parting rays yet illumined the west,
All Nature was hushed in a quiet profound,
And exquisite grandeur was gathering around.

'Twas fair as an Eden, yet lovelier still
Grew the scene, as ye gazed over valley and hill,
'Twas beauty entrancing from cloudlet to stream,
As the painter might wish, or the poet might dream.

Yes, Nature spoke volumes in proof of her God,
From the golden tipp'd hills to the daisy deck'd sod,
No sceptic would dare have profaned such a scene,
By denying the Hand that so lavish had been.

THE POET'S WREATH.

Yet bright as the scene and surpassingly fair,
'Twas greatly enhanced by a vision more rare ;
A picture of innocence, beauty and love,
Which well might have ranked with the angels above.

In a secret recess of this beautiful spot,
Where the cares of the world might have well been forgot,
Or the over-charged heart might have hoped to endure,
Its own bitter grief undisturbed and secure.

Close sheltered and hid from the gaze of the rude,
With a sorrow too sacred for such to intrude,
Knelt a beautiful maiden, imploring of Heaven,
That strength in this hour of her grief might be given.

'Tis the old bitter tale of a broken young heart,
Compell'd from earth's fondest and dearest to part,
A proud father's love for his gold had decreed,
That her fond trusting heart should thus languish and bleed.

She had lov'd in her early days wisely and well,
With a depth of affection no language can tell,
And the now sainted mother had blessed ere she died,
The worthy young swain as he knelt by her side.

But evil days came, and her Edwin was poor,
And the proud father could not such evil endure,
So boasting that filial care was his pride,
Her prayers and her tears he most firmly denied.

While one far advanced both in years and in sin,
With his gold and his title fain hoped he might win
Her fond loving heart, with her form so divine :
Proud dreamer, dream on ; she can never be thine.

She had asked but for once to meet Edwin again,
That meeting was fraught with much sorrow and pain ;
No mortal e'er knew what had passed in that hour,
But angels could whisper of love's binding power.

With his fond widowed mother poor Edwin had gone,
From his home and his country to try and live on,
But had faded and died on a cold foreign shore,
And the poor mother wrote that her son was no more.

This morning had brought her the tidings of death,
And also the words of his last whispered breath ;
Tell Laura I go to the realms of the fair
To watch for her coming and wait for her there.

She had read these last words till her eyes had grown dim,
Till she felt that her soul was but waiting for him ;
She had felt her great sorrow too deeply to pray,
Till she found her way here at the close of the day.

Long and earnestly prayed she that God would forgive,
Even those who had made it so dreary to live :
While a loving voice whispered tho' faintly yet near,
"We shall meet yet again, darling, be of good cheer."

She rose and was comforted ; darkness was past,
Hope's star o'er her soul shone triumphant at last ;
She knew and she felt that her sun would yet rise,
To shine more resplendent 'neath happier skies.

Time pass'd, and the father, with mistaken care,
Thought it best that his child for her change should prepare,
For the wealthy old lover had bought with his gold
The hand, but the heart still refused to be sold.

She had never been asked, she had never said No !
Nor ever consented that this should be so ;
She had never deceived him, by word or by look,
They knew her no more than a sacred sealed book.

She had smiled never yet since the day she had said,
Farewell to the one who now ranked with the dead,
But had patiently borne all her trials and care,
Since the day she had found such a solace in prayer.

Yet they marked the slow step once so graceful and light,
And the sad dreamy look of those eyes once so bright :
The bloom on her cheek was fast passing away,
Yet they smiled as they spoke of her bridal array.

For the wealthy old baronet freely had spent
His gold for the grand and much-hoped-for event,
And the father, whose pride was now pampered and fed,
Never dreamt how the heart of his daughter had bled.

And thus they went on and the bridal eve came,
They thought her no worse, but of course much the same ;
They knew not how slowly yet surely that heart
With sorrow was breaking, and soon they must part.

She had begged to retire rather early to rest,
And the father had whispered, as fondly he pressed
The child who had been his sole comfort in sorrow,
" My darling, I hope you'll be better to-morrow."

She lovingly lingered and held him a while,
And back to her beautiful face came the smile,
And her look was so earnest he dreamt not of sorrow,
As she echoed his words, " I'll be better to-morrow."

The morrow's sun rose without blemish or blot,
They call'd for the bride but she answered them not,
They hastened to rouse her, and chide her long sleep,
Ah! well might they tremble, and silently weep.

They caught the last smile, they saw the last breath,
Heard a name fondly breathed 'mid the throbbings of death,
That name was the fondest, the dearest and last,
And with him her freed spirit now joyously passed.

Ah! who will deny that our loved ones are near,
Our sorrows to lighten our spirits to cheer,
Oh! who would not wish when this earth-life is past.
Like Laura, to meet with the loved ones at last?

RICH AND POOR.

(Suggested by the Cotton Strike.)

"Sell all thou hast and give it to the poor."

Earth held not in all her proud palaces one
Who more for the poor of his country had done
Than He who thus answer'd the urgent request
Of one who most earnestly sought to be blest.

No doubt he had waited for many a day,
Intending, if Jesus should pass in his way,
To pray the Great Teacher more plainly to state
How he best might secure an eternal estate.

Most anxious, indeed, the young nobleman felt,
As earth's Master approached—for before Him he knelt,
And in touching humility offer'd his prayer,
Regardless of all save that Jesus was there.

He pleads that from youth he has kept the commands—
Hear this ye that boast of your houses and lands—
He led a life equal to many of you,
And yet he inquired what more he could do.

The Saviour looked on him with pitying love,
As He read him his claim to the mansions above ;
One sin yet remained—he must leave even this—
Ere the bliss that he sighed for could ever be his.

He must part from his gold—he had lov'd it too well ;
This last darling idol He bids him expel ;
'Twas a snare to this rich one—the poor it might save,
For want opens many a premature grave.

He offers him treasures that pass not away
In exchange for the dross He has doom'd to decay ;
In tenderest pity implores him to choose—
Will he wisely accept it or madly refuse?

One moment of thrilling suspense, then he cast
One look at his Saviour, his fondest and last ;
Then slowly and sadly he passed on his way.—
We shall meet him no more till the last final day.

We may hear of him then ; it might be that at last,
When the charm of his riches for ever had pass'd ;
When wealth offered nothing his peace to restore,
The reign of his golden god then might be o'er.

How many like him, whose possessions are great,
Run the same fearful risk of his uncertain fate?
How many who, but for this one fatal sin,
Need fear not, or fail, heaven's treasures to win?

Can those who are seeking the poor to oppress
Ever hope that this Saviour their efforts will bless?
Do they fondly imagine their gold will prevail
'Gainst the honest man's prayer or his children's sad wail?

Oh! ye who have power for good or for ill,
Remember the aching hearts waiting your will;
Forget not that He who hath bless'd you in store
Hath also commanded, "Deal well with the poor."

Yet thousands are wanting the bread ye can give
In return for the labour by which they must live;
In mercy then save from this direst of ills—
Cheer the heart of your country and open your mills.

They ask but their right, and ye know it is true:
Your Bible instructs you to pay what is due:
Ye reap a rich harvest from their honest gains.
Then why seek to force them in fetters and chains

To work at your bid, at the price ye would give?
On which in most cases they could not well live;
Many barely exist, ye could not call it life,
And yet ye would strengthen this ruinous strife.

Hard enough is the life of a poor working man,
Who day after day must toil hard as he can,
Whose nights find him wearied in body and brain,
Till nature exhausted sinks under the strain.

And yet ye would take from this overworked man
A part of his hardly-earned wages, and plan
How best to compel him your vile ends to meet—
Starvation must bring him in chains to you feet.

Oh ! Englishmen, blight not your country's fair fame,
Prove yourselves truly worthy of England's proud name ;
Delay not, but hasten your people to save,
Or many ere long will find rest in the grave.

For fathers are sinking, they'll soon pass away,
And mothers are leaving us day after day,
While innocent children are pining for bread—
How can you withold it and raise your proud head ?

Ye suffering workers, still patiently wait,
There are hearts that mourn deeply your underserved fate ;
Suffer peacefully on, oh ! raise not a hand
'Gainst those who have wrought this distress in our land.

Ye have honour'd your name, oh ! stain it not now,
Not long 'neath the yoke of oppression ye'll bow ;
Not long shall they trample you under their feet—
Remember they, too, have a judgment to meet.

Then plead your sad case at the bar of that One,
Who ordered that justice and right should be done ;
Then when this and all future struggles are o'er,
'Twill add to your bliss that on earth ye were poor.

IN MEMORIAM.—WM. BURY, ESQ.

"Nay, Death, they are not thine."

They are not thine, proud cruel death,
    Those lov'd ones gone from earth ;
Not thine the soul's diviner breath,
    Not thine that holier birth.

The pure and sacred flame of love,
    That spark of life divine ;
The theme of angel songs above
    Can never, death, be thine.

The secret, hidden force of life,
    It were not thine to sever ;
Beyond these shades of mortal strife,
    Its waves roll on for ever.

Not thine the wondrous mystic power
    That renders life so fair,
That brightens earth's dark weary hour,
    And lightens every care.

Not thine the hope and dream of years,
    From waiting hearts to sever ;
Beyond the tide of human tears
    They'll meet again for ever.

The fondly lov'd, to memory dear,
    That round our hearts entwine,
Though vacant now their places here,
    Still, death, they are not thine.

We see beyond thy frowning tide
    A world of beauty rare,
And they who once on earth have died
    Still smile upon us there.

We hear across thy stormy swell,
    From that immortal shore,
The glad re-echo, " All is well !
    We live for evermore."

Yes, death, they live on happier plains,
    Those gems of life divine ;
And while a God eternal reigns,
    They never can be thine.

JEALOUSY.

AN IMPROMPTU.

Beware, O beware ! of this dangerous sin,
    Give it never a place in your heart ;
Check at once and for ever, if peace ye would win,
    Its fatal and poisonous dart.

More homes have been wreck'd than our records have shown
    By its hateful and treacherous wile ;
More hopes have been blighted, more discord been sown,
    More hearts turned from virtue to guile.

It has severed the fondest, the dearest of ties,
  And blasted much innocent fame ;
Stained many a soul with sin's deepest dyes,
  Brought ruin to many a proud name.

Our prisons have held many fondly lov'd sons,
  Yea, and daughters once owned with much pride,
Who, but for the poison that jealousy runs,
  Had never thus languished and died.

Many aged and trembling, with none to protect,
  Dishonoured have passed to the grave ;
While the young and the lovely have often been wrecked,
  Overwhelm'd by the same cruel wave.

Oh ! the tears and the sighs, and the heartrending cries,
  That our winds have borne on in their sweep :
Methinks could they pierce the celestial skies,
  That for once even angels might weep.

Then shun, brother mortal, this ruinous sin,
  Turn the dark loathsome foe from thy heart ;
Check at once and for ever its tiniest spring,
  Ere thou fall by its venomous dart.

A CONTRAST.

The New York "Sun" estimates that there are 10,000 working women receiving wages so low that they must embrace vice, apply for charity, or starve. And yet, one church society is erecting a cathedral to cost $7,000,000. The Rev. Dr. Dix, pastor of Trinity Church, receives $20,000 per year for preaching the gospel.

What Gospel I should like to know
    Can Dr. Dix be preaching ;
Is all this pomp and gilded show,
    The outcome of his teaching.
Does he believe a costly wall
    Of architectural beauty ;
Will please the Father, God of all,
    Instead of saintly duty.

Suppose we take this man of pride,
    This richly-portioned preacher ;
And place him for awhile beside
    The Galilean teacher.
Minutely scan the lives of each
    Ye honest-hearted sages,
Compare the principles they teach,
    And then compare the wages.

One teaches from the mountain's brow,
    'Mid nature's lovely dells ;
In fields were golden corn sheaves bow,
    And by the wayside wells.
Sometimes upon the angry wave,
    While thunders crash around :
And sometimes by the silent grave,
    This Man of God is found.

The other 'neath a costly dome,
  Of grand artistic beauty,
Where scarce the poor ill-clad may roam,
  To breathe their vows of duty.
With sheltered head and cushioned tread,
  And fashion's glare around him,
Where wealth's proud idol rears her head,
  There golden coils have bound him.

The gentle Galilean knew
  The want of home and bread;
And often when the night winds blew
  Could nowhere lay His head.
Night's shades have often o'er Him furl'd
  When bow'd in bitter sorrow,
And yet a faithless, cruel world,
  He blessed on each to-morrow.

The other flattered, pampered, fed,
  Dwells in a lordly hall;
On downy pillow rests his head,
  While wealth presides o'er all.
No weary footsteps mark his way,
  Night's dews fall not on him,
But comforts flow from day to day,
  In plenteous streams for him.

Poor Jesus always might be found
  Amongst the poor and lowly;
No matter by what fetters bound,
  Degraded or unholy.
He never shunned the fevered bed,
  Or passed the house of sorrow:
But by His sainty lustre shed
  Gems of a happier morrow.

The other takes the higher ground,
  Where fashion's lead is strongest ;
Where sumptuous ease is ever found,
  There will he tarry longest.
But when the pestilential fear
  Is raging far and wide,
When death and danger lurketh near,
  He kindly steps aside.

I wonder has the Doctor taught
  Those lessons from the mountain ;
The richest, purest, gems of thought
  From inspiration's fountain ;
Or does he to his hearers show
  Their duty to their neighbour,
Or brand the sin of those who go
  And trample honest labour.

The Gospel Jesus gave the world
  Centres in one grand duty ;
Which practised by Himself unfurl'd
  A life of rarest beauty.
The golden rule if taught to-day,
  With such examples leading,
Would prove one great redeeming ray
  This darkened world is needing.

Would God this ray of Gospel light
  Might break into a flame ;
And chase this dark Egyptian night
  Which wraps the world in shame.
Would heaven some mighty force might shake
  Those shepherds of the fold,
And bid them from their slumbers wake,
  And break their gods of gold.

But stay my muse, that day is nigh,
  'Tis even in the dawn,
Humanity's despairing cry
  Has reached the eternal throne.
And back has come a mighty wave,
  Which sweeps from cloud to sod,
Destined this ruined world to save,
  And give it back to God.

Not long shall trampled women slave
  In sin and shame and sorrow ;
The grand redress for which they crave
  Comes with that brighter morrow.
Not long the starving child of earth,
  Shall plead but to be fed ;
That God who gave the creature birth,
  Gave also honest bread.

Oppression's reign is nearly run,
  It's harvest nearly past,
The hidden Gospel's welcome sun
  Will flood the earth at last.
And 'neath those fertilizing rays,
  Shall blossom lives of beauty :
While brighter, happier, holier days,
  Reward their honest duty.

Hail then, ye noble-hearted crew,
  Ye workers in the slums ;
From worlds beyond where all is true,
  Your inspiration comes.
On, in the cause of truth and right,
  On, for ye cannot fail :
Still on, for 'gainst this evil night
  Ye must and shall prevail.

"SHE'S ONLY GONE TO SLEEP."

DEDICATED TO FRED.

Yes, baby, sister's gone to sleep,
    Earth cannot wake her, never;
Where angel children cease to weep,
    She's gone to dwell for ever.

Pain cannot reach thy sister there,
    No wrong can mar her beauty;
Taught by the angels ever fair,
    She'll learn an angel's duty.

They'll teach her gentle unstain'd soul
    The love that bears for ever;
And long as earthly years may roll,
    She will forget thee never.

Soon will her tender soul o'erflow
    With love for human kind;
And will she not that love bestow
    On those she left behind?

Yes, Fred, my boy, that angel child,
    By heavenly guidance fitted;
May lead thy steps through earth's dark wild,
    By ruling love permitted.

Should length of years be thine below,
    To brave life's stormy ocean;
Oh, be it thine to trust and show
    A beautiful devotion.

Be thine a noble true resolve,
  To so fulfil life's duty ;
That long as endless years revolve,
  Thy soul may grow in beauty.

Thus baby sister's earthly sleep
  Though now a bitter sorrow ;
May bring to those who mourn and weep
  A fair and bright to-morrow.

IN MEMORIAM.

IMPROMPTU POEM WRITTEN ON THE DEATH OF ALEXANDER HARGREAVES.

"The young and the beautiful die."

In the bloom of youth and beauty,
  In the sweet springtide of life,
From the post of honoured duty,
  Called to leave earth's weary strife.

Ere the cares of life could meet him,
  Or his soul with sorrow bend,
Angel friends with pleasure greet him,
  To the joys which ne'er shall end.

Ere his tender heart could sorrow,
   O'er the cold world's bitter chill,
Heaven's eternal bright to-morrow,
   Fills his soul with pleasure still.

Ere affliction long had known him
   Ere his soul could weary be,
God's most tender love is shown him,
   He from future ills is free.

Happy youth, thy life in heaven,
   Purer, brighter, still shall grow,
To thy noble soul is given,
   Heights of rapture yet to know.

May one sunny ray of gladness,
   From thy soothing presence near,
Reach the hearts that yet in sadness,
   Mourn because thou art not here.

May the mother who caressed thee,
   And the weeping ones so dear,
Know that God who thus hath blessed thee,
   Soon will chase their every tear.

May the love that ever bound thee,
   Like a halo circle o'er,
Till again the lov'd have found thee,
   On the bright eternal shore.

THE MUSE.

[On the Twenty-third of St. Matthew.]

Wearily pondering over the past,
   So laden with sorrow and care,
With every vestige of sky overcast,
   And a fast-yielding sense of despair.

Weary of weeping the dreary long day,
   And dreading each long weary night,
And weary of watching through life's gloomy way,
   For only one glimmer of light.

Weary of pity from those who might save
   From gathering darkness around,
If only the tide of humanity's wave,
   In their cold selfish hearts could be found.

Weary, yes, weary of life and its care,
   And tired of earth's bitter scorn;
Oh! Why in a world so entrancingly fair
   Should wrong and oppression be borne?

Why should the poor toiler petition and pray
   That justice and right should be given?
Can the gold-loving Christian tyrant to-day
   Believe in the justice of heaven?

Sure not, or the words of his Saviour would teach
   His cold selfish heart to relent:
For does He not judgments most terrible preach
   'Gainst those on such tyranny bent?

Does he not, in His anger, denounce those who pray
  And boast of the tithes they have given ;
Who tell Him how much they have paid, by the way,
  To open the kingdom of heaven ?

Does He bless the oppressors who burden the poor
  With sorrows they cannot well bear ,
And answer most readily certain and sure,
  Their long hypocritical prayer.

Or, does He not rather condemn them in wrath,
  If his terrible language must tell ;
And point out the end of their gold-laden path
  And show their tyrannical hell ?

Poor, crucified Jesus ! Thy time-honoured name,
  They stain and dishonour it yet ;
Thy beautiful life and Thy glorious fame,
  In the worship of self they forget.

The whited sepulchres are fair to behold
  Though filled with contention and pride ;
And many still worship the image of gold,
  While preaching the Saviour who died.

Much evil is done in Thy glorious name,
  And done by Thy worshippers too ;
They put Thee again to Thy once open shame,
  Then boast that they honour Thee true.

Dear Jesus, if still Thou hast power to defend
  The down-trodden poor of our land,
We pray Thee a convoy of angels to send,
  And free us from tyranny's band.

Redeem Thy fair name from the dark dreary stain;
　Which has dimm'd its bright lustre too long;
Unveil Thy illustrious self once again,
　And chase from our midst this deep wrong.

Bring down all this arrogance, pride, and deceit,
　Restore Thy lost beautiful life;
Let Christian honour and honesty meet,
　And end this un-Christian strife.

Oh! Then shall Thy name, like the sun in our sphere,
　Shed a halo o'er life's darkened way,
And lead through the gloom of our pilgrimage here,
　To the realms of a glorious day.

IN MEMORIAM.

Mrs. John Bury.

Friend after friend departs;
Who has not lost a friend?

Another friend has left me,
Long trusted, tried, and true,
But one whose noble virtues
Were known to but a few;
Yet 'mongst that favour'd number,
Through all life's changing scene,
To me unchanging ever
That faithful heart has been.

Not in life's sunny morning,
When, like a poet's dream,
With golden skies above me,
Life seem'd one beauteous stream ;
But when those skies have darken'd,
And tempests gather'd round,
True as the stars of heaven,
That friend was ever found.

When summer friends have left me,
To bear the gloom alone,
When cruel slight and coldness
My tortur'd heart has known ;
When hope had well-nigh left me,
And faith's bright star had paled—
In nature's darkest sorrow
Her friendship never fail'd.

And now, with earth-life ended,
Its cares for ever past,
The sweet reward of harvest
Is her's to reap at last.
Each earthly deed of kindness,
Each generous loving thought,
Each faithful act of duty,
With richest fruit is fraught.

Farewell, old friend, I mourn not
Thy glad release from earth,
While angels bid thee welcome,
Thou child of happier birth,
Thou well hast won thy laurels,
And nobly earn'd thy rest ;
Then take the joys before thee,
And rank among the blest.

'Tis not for long I'll miss thee,
The time for me will come,
When, like some wearied pilgrim,
I'll reach my spirit's home.
Home! Let me close my farewell
With that word on my ear,
It wakes a thousand echoes
From lov'd ones—over there.

ONLY A PAUPER.

She had walked from the refuge, a weary two mile,
And was leaning for rest on the old broken stile,
Where in happier days she had lingered with one
Who had long from the world and its sorrows been gone.

From the dearly lov'd spot she could look on the scene
Where the gambols and play of her girlhood had been,
Where the lov'd and the loving had wandered so free,
Ever dreaming how blissful their future should be.

While gazing around her in sorrow and pain,
The tide of the past seemed to roll back again;
And the veil that had gathered in sorrow's dark hour
Give way 'neath the spell of some mystical power.

Fond memory awoke from the sleep of long years,
And opened the fount of her long pent-up tears;
And as visions of beauty and happiness passed,
The heart's deepest waters were troubled at last.

Long and sadly she wept as the lovely scenes fled,
As she gazed on the forms of her long-hidden dead,
While echoing back on the tide as it fell,
Came the voices of loved ones remembered so well.

Ah! this is an hour when life is but weak,
When the slightest rude touch will the tender strings break;
When the heart, now already too full to endure,
Needs little indeed its last throb to ensure.

While the poor aged mourner, thus sorely in need,
Sat silently waiting for strength to proceed,
A lady approached her, adorned with much pride,
While a sweet little girl skipped along by her side.

The child's tender nature, unchill'd by the world,
Would there a most beautiful trait have unfurled,
But the world-fashioned mamma stoop'd gently to say,
"She's only a pauper! My darling, don't stay."

The old lady heard them, but none would have thought
Of the deep, subtle mischief those idle words wrought:
Such words are most cutting, most cruel, and sore,
Did we know but their power, we should breathe them no
    more.

Time sped, and the poor, weary pilgrim was laid
At the house of a friend, where a visit she'd paid;
Prostrated with weakness, o'ercome with distress,
But praying that heaven their kindness would bless.

As matters grew worse, and her illness increased,
A medical man was entreated at least
To visit her once and pronounce on her state,
But he answered with scorn that "A pauper must wait."

He had those on his hands whose lives were worth saving,
And Lady Van Dell for her child was now craving ;
And offered much gold could he save her this sorrow,
The pauper must surely then wait for the morrow.

The morrow came round, and the doctor was there,
But the pauper was far from his kindness and care ;
She had died just an hour before, whispering, "They come !
The angels of glory, to welcome me home."

. . . .

A fair little form had been laid down to rest
'Mid the dark gloomy splendour of all that was best,
But the poor bereaved mother could turn not away
From the spot where her only, her darling one lay.

She was lingering still when another slow tread
Impell'd her to raise her proud, beautiful head ;
'Twas the Lady Van Dell who now piteously cried,
"Would God, like the pauper, I too had but died!"

Strange meeting ! The same little darling we saw,
Whose mamma forbade her a kindness to show
To a poor honest pauper in nature's dark hour—
"Oh ! Death, thou art mighty, we own to thy power."

"The wealthy can never compel thee to wait,
Or urge thee to spare them this one common fate ;
Their gold cannot tempt thee themselves to pass by,
Or they only would live, and the paupers would die.

"But, in the beyond, where distinctions are not,
Where names shall be rid of this dark, loathsome blot,
Our paupers shall wander, unfettered and free,
And the badge that has marked them shall perish with thee."

IN MEMORIAM.—EDWIN WAUGH.

"Death is the mightier second birth,
The unveiling of the soul."

All hail ! emancipated soul,
   Well ended thy probation,
Not now shall earth's discordant roll
   Impede thy inspiration.

For clearer, sweeter, richer far,
   Where kindred souls are dwelling ;
Where brightly gleams thy rising star,
   Thy music still is swelling.

There in that holier, happier sphere,
   Where earth's great poets gather :
Thy soul shall comprehend more clear
   The great eternal Father.

There after all earth's weary round,
    The toil and care and weeping;
There bloometh on celestial ground
    An harvest worth thy reaping.

We speak of death as though, alas!
    'Twere nought but gloom and sorrow;
Forgetting 'tis the only pass
    To that unclouded morrow.

Be thine the task, thou master mind,
    By purer inspiration,
To teach earth's wearied how to find
    The surest consolation.

In honour of thy glorious birth,
    The light now thine, bestow it:
In memory of thy life on earth,
    Inspire some humbler poet.

'Twas thine whilst here to chase away
    The gloom of sin and sorrow;
And point beyond earth's darkening day
    To God's eternal morrow.

So be it still; lead on, till we
    Like thee shall cross death's river;
Till earth-life pass and then with thee
    We'll meet, and meet for ever.

REMEMBER THE POOR.

The night was a bitter one, piercing and cold,
Just the night when stern poverty's pages unfold,
When the rich may rejoice o'er their coffers well filled,
While the poor in their homes are half frozen and chilled.

When forth from her cosy warm home with delight,
Out in the cold went the lovely Miss Bright,
Bent on a mission of mercy and love,
Which sure would have honoured an angel above.

Her father had long been the pastor and friend
Of a neat little village not far from Lane End,
Where two years before he had laid down to rest
The dear little wife who had made his home blest.

But yet she had left him this daughter most fair,
And lovingly charged her his labour to share,
With strictest injunctions the poor to befriend,
Whose comfort and welfare had been her sole end.

And faithfully had she fulfilled the request,
In the hearts she had gladdened and homes she had blest;
Not only wise counsels of love did she give,
But in teaching them how she had helped them to live.

Each Christmas she spent in distributing free
To the comfort of those not so favoured as she,
And hearts had been turned from earth's darkness to light,
Through the unselfish care of the noble Miss Bright.

And this was the night when her visits fell due,
Besides she had promised to call for Miss Frew,
Who long had protested no good could she see
In visiting paupers and taking them tea.

So with basket well laden with all she required
She boldly step'd forward, nor fainted nor tired,
Till she and her friend entered Wellington Court,
Where liv'd just a few of the better poor sort.

The first call they made was on poor Widow Lee,
With her invalid son sitting snugly at tea,
In a home which for neatness and cleanliness too,
Pleased the eye of the aristocratic Miss Frew.

When greetings were passed and the visitors sat,
It was pleasing to listen to Mrs. Lee's chat,
As she briefly recounted the kindness of those
Whose generous spirit had lessened her woes.

"And really, Miss Bright," said the widow with joy,
"I have cause to rejoice for the sake of my boy,
The only one left to a mother's fond heart;
How I shrank from the thought that perhaps we might part.

But the doctor declares now the fever's quite gone,
He'll soon be again my stout little John,
Then I shall rejoicingly lift up my head,
And once more be able to earn my own bread.

They relieved Widow Lee, and with many more thanks
She bade them "good-bye," and they called on Miss Banks,
A poor aged cripple who liv'd quite alone,
But whose Martyr-like patience Miss Bright had long known.

They surprised the old dame in the midst of a song,
As with one stick in hand she was hobbling along,
And putting to rights a few things by the way,
For Miss Banks had received many presents that day.

And well might she sing for her bread it was sure,
And for some time at least she could not be called poor ;
So bidding Miss Bright and her friend take a seat,
She spread out before them her wonderful treat.

There was butter and sugar, and bread by the pound,
With a nice pot of jam—how it made her heart bound—
Such luxuries had not been always her fare,
She felt quite as proud as if wife of the mayor.

"And besides this, Miss Bright," said she, quickly as
    thought,
"Quite a good stock of coal I had this morning brought,
I shall live like a princess, of that I am sure,
Heaven's blessings on those who are kind to the poor."

She rambled and chatted, and talked with such power,
Miss Bright and her friend never thought of the hour,
Till the faithful old clock struck the time on his bell,
Then they bade her "good night," and wished her quite
    well.

One or two houses more and their work was well done,
Their basket was emptied, their pleasure well won ;
And Miss Frew was conquered and ventured to say,
More real enjoyment was gained in this way.

Since then she has laboured, incessantly too,
And many are blessing the name of Miss Frew,
Who thinks it no longer beneath her to be
Seen visiting paupers and taking them tea.

Many more have since joined them and find themselves blest,
In visiting those who are sorely distrest,
Though in creed they may vary of this we are sure,
They lend but to God what they give to the poor.

IN MEMORIAM.—MRS. NEWELL.

"There is no death."

It is not death, oh no not death,
  'Tis but another stage of life ;
'Tis but the yielding mortal breath,
  The end of earth's sad weary strife.
One step towards the grand ascent,
  One scene in life's great drama past,
The soul on progress ever bent,
  Has pass'd the bounds of earth at last.
    It is not death,
    Oh no not death.

With death we claim no kith or kin,
    We know the God-like spark within
Howe'er the tide of life may turn,
    Shall ever round its centre burn.
And though obscured by shadows here,
    The light from some more perfect sphere
Shall guide its feeble flickering glow
    Safe through the shades of earth's deep woe.
        It is not death,
          Oh no not death.

To death we give the mortal form,
    In which this earthly stage is run ;
While far beyond earth's wildest storm,
    A better life is just begun.
Where under more congenial skies,
    We live and love for evermore,
And taught by purer souls we rise
    To higher glories still before.
        It is not death,
          Oh no not death.

Did we believe our loved and dear,
    With whom we held sweet converse here,
Had left our hearth and homes below,
    And pass'd to endless joy or woe,
And we this mortal life must wait,
    To know their dark or happy fate :
While loving hearts in anguish bleed,
    Oh this were cruel death indeed.
        Yes this were death,
          And death indeed.

IN MEMORIAM.

Albert Dobson.—Over There.

'Tis in truth a world of sorrow,
　　Though so beautiful and fair ;
Smiles to-day, maybe to-morrow
　　Tears of bitter grief or care.
But a world of richer beauty
　　Opens to our faith and prayer ;
Home of angel-love and duty,
　　Waits for each one—over there.

Here our heart's best love has centred
　　On some darling one most near ;
Death our peaceful home has entered,
　　Taking just that one so dear.
But beyond the grave's dark portal,
　　Where we laid the casket fair,
Blooms the gem of life immortal,
　　Lives our lov'd one—over there.

Here we meet but meet to sever,
　　Friends are passing fast away ;
One by one they're gone for ever,
　　Leaving blanks by life's dull way.
But we see them as they gather
　　One by one in realms more fair,
Children of one happy Father,
　　In His mansions—over there.

Here we kneel around one altar,
　　Seeking guidance through life's day ;
And our spirits often falter
　　O'er earth's rough and toilsome way.

But when prayers and tears are ended,
    And our spirits free from care,
We shall find all have but tended
    To our rapture—over there.

Rouse, ye mourners, from your sorrow,
    Look beyond these shades of earth,
And behold that holier morrow,
    Where your loving one has birth,
Enter those celestial portals,
    Open to your faith and prayer;
Search among those bright immortals,
    Ye shall find him—over there.

IN MEMORIAM.

ALICE HIGHAM.

"For ever with the Lord."

For ever, for ever, at rest with her God,
    Away from this earth's dreary night,
Not under the cold, cheerless, pitiless sod,
    But away to the regions of light.

For ever at rest with the lov'd who had passed,
    From her sight by this life's darkened way,
But the darkness is chased from her spirit at last,
    By the light of God's glorious day.

For ever at rest from affliction and pain,
    Where sorrows may never more roll,
To the harvest of love she had liv'd to attain,
    In the beautiful home of the soul.

For ever at rest from the world and its cares,
    Where many now pray but to be
In the land of her earliest—holiest prayers,
    Blest spirit, why weep we for thee?

For ever beyond thee, proud Death, is that soul,
    Thy conquests belong but to earth,
Thy merciless waves are forbidden to roll
    On the shores of that holier birth.

For ever with angels, whose guardian care
    Shall ever lead upward and on,
To scenes more entrancing, more wondrously rare,
    While still higher beauties roll on.

For ever with Jesus, whose Name she professed,
    Whose beautiful life was her guide,
Who called the tried Spirit so early to rest,
    Away from this earth's chilling tide.

For ever, dear sainted one, we too, would pray,
    May we be thus gloriously blest,
May we, when our Spirits have left the cold clay,
    Have earned the same heaven's sweet rest.

HYMN ON THE DEATH OF ELI HIGHAM, JUNIOR.

Tune—"Shall we meet beyond the river."

We shall meet beyond the river,
　When these sad farewells are o'er;
We shall join the lov'd for ever,
　On a brighter, fairer shore.

Chorus.

　We shall meet, we shall meet,
　　We shall meet and love for ever;
　We shall meet and love for ever,
　　When these sad farewells are o'er.

We shall know why all this sorrow,—
　All this darkness by the way;
And before that bright to-morrow,
　All these clouds shall pass away.
　　　　　　　We shall meet, &c.

Here are breaking hearts around us,
　Funeral's dark and solemn shade;
And bright loving forms that bound us,
　In the earth's cold arms are laid.
　　　　　　　We shall meet, &c.

Many brave and noble hearted,
　Whom we could not choose to spare,
Have like sunny dreams departed,
　Leaving life less bright and fair.
　　　　　　　We shall meet, &c.

Not the aged, worn and weary,
  Who for death would gladly pray,
But the young, the bright and cheery,
  These the soonest pass away.
              We shall meet, &c.

Noble brother, though we mourn thee,
  And thy genial presence miss,
Angel hands with gems adorn thee,
  In that sunny land of bliss.
              We shall meet, &c.

Though thy voice no longer soundeth
  In the songs we sing with tears,
Yet thy soul's rich joy aboundeth
  In the music of the spheres.
              We shall meet, &c.

Weary mourners, cease your sorrow,
  Look beyond death's dreary tide;
Safe in Heaven's bright to-morrow,
  Lives your loving one that died.
              We shall meet, &c.

Yes we'll meet, and meet for ever,
  On a brighter, fairer shore,
Where not even death can sever,
  And farewells shall all be o'er.
              We shall meet, &c.

A VOICE FROM BEYOND.

IN MEMORY OF THE LATE MR. DAVID ORMEROD.

"In Heaven above, where all is love,
Ther'll be no more sorrow there."

No sorrows we know in these realms of delight,
   No grief ever darkens our home,
No scenes of distress our pleasures can blight,
   In happy contentment we roam.

No parting with husband, or father so dear,
   No severing friendship's sweet tie,
No sudden or lingering death do we fear,
   We live but we never can die.

No dreary procession of funeral shade,
   No widow or sorrowing heir,
No desolate orphans in heaven are made,
   We know not a shadow of care.

No tears ever fall, no sighs ever tell
   The sorrows that break the fond heart;
We hear not the tones of your deep passing bell
   As they echo "Ye mortals must part."

No graves with their beautiful flowerets so fair,
   Or the ever green tear-bedeck'd sod,
No wail of distress ever floats on the air,
   In this beautiful City of God.

We live in a world most transcendently fair,
   No clouds ever darken our sky,
No hearts are here broken by grief and despair,
   Our friends never languish and die.

Our sun never yields to the darkness of night,
    Our days are all balmy and fair,
Our flowers for ever are blooming and bright,
    And angel songs float on the air.

We meet and rejoice with the friends who have pass'd
    From earth and its sorrows away,
The bond of our friendship for ever shall last,
    Our pleasures can never decay.

We learn of the angels their beautiful life,
    We join in their beautiful song,
We rest from all suffering, sorrow and strife,
    A happy and glorified throng.

Poor mourner of earth, never yield to despair,
    Thy lov'd one is happy and free,
Somewhere in God's mansions so wondrously fair,
    He lovingly waiteth for thee.

IN MEMORIAM.

Miss Annie Williams.

"When and Where."

When life's sad fitful dream is o'er,
    Its cares and sorrows past;
When cruel death can never more
    His darkening shadow cast;
When sever'd hearts so rudely torn
    Have throbb'd their last deep pain;
When dawns the grand eternal morn—
    Then we shall meet again.

When fond farewells have all been said,
When tears no longer fall ;
When earth's cold, narrow, silent bed
Receives our earthly all :
When softly o'er our spirits steal
Those chords of holier strain :
When once-lov'd hands again we feel—
Then we shall meet again.

Where worlds revolve more glorious far
Than aught of thine, oh, earth ;
Where each transplendent radiant star
Reveals some happier birth ;
Where blend the purest gems of thought,
With music's richest strain ;
Where hearts with sweetest joys are fraught—
There we shall meet again.

Where cloudless skies and fadeless flowers
Make one eternal spring,
Where through the happy golden hours
Familiar voices ring ;
Where beam the smiles we lov'd so well,
That lighten'd earth's dull pain ;
'Mid scenes of which no muse can tell—
There we shall meet again.

Thou bright ascended happy soul,
If Highest Wisdom will
Sometimes 'mid earth's dark dreary roll,
Be near our spirits still ;
And teach us from those realms above,
How we may best attain
That home of wondrous joy and love,
Where all may meet again.

DR. CLAYTON.

IN MEMORIAM.

"We shall meet, but we shall miss him."

One by one, our friends are passing
Quickly from this mortal sphere ;
Old familiar forms have vanished,
True and loyal, fond and dear ;
Eyes that shone with love's own brightness,
Hearts that throbb'd with love's sweet thrill,
Hands that minister'd in kindness,
Now are silent, cold, and still.

But of all familiar faces,
None shall we so sadly miss
As the Doctor's well-known features,
And that genial smile of his.
Foremost of our willing helpers,
Prompt and ready at each call,
Full of noble deeds of kindness ;
Now, alas, we'll miss them all.

How they'll miss him as they gather
Lov'd ones round his vacant chair,
How fond memory oft will linger
O'er the scenes that centre there ;
Scenes of home life, richly blending
Days that seem'd too fair to last ;
Hopes more bright than summer sunlight,
All like sunny dreams are past.

When the Council friends assemble,
How they'll miss his honest greet;
And in school or sanctuary,
When the worshippers shall meet;
In the mansion or the cottage,
Soothing oft some anxious care;
In the sufferer's silent chamber—
We shall miss him everywhere.

But, enough of earth's dark sorrow;
Turn we to a brighter side,
Someone whispers, oh, how sweetly,
Look beyond death's gloomy tide;
There rich scenes of rarest beauty
Meet him with a glad surprise,
And a grand reunion gathers
In that home where nothing dies.

CONTENTS.

	PAGE.
A Short Dedication, in Memoriam, Benj. Hargreaves, Esq.	5
In Memoriam—Benjamin Harrison, Esq. ...	6
Preface	7
The Angel's Wreath	9
A Wasted Life	12
A Sad Story	17
The Suicide's Grave ...	25
My Childhood's Home	27
In Memoriam—Duke of Albany	28
Pity Me Not	30
Song—The Drunkard's Dying Child	31
Song—The Father's Vow ...	33
In Memory of the Lifeboat Crew ...	34
A Plea for the Unemployed	35
One by One	37
No Creed	38
Reverie, Written in Oak Hill Grounds ...	40
In Memoriam—Mrs. W. Smith	42
Song of the Weary ...	44
Song of Hope	45
Can this be True?	46
To the Memory of Lord Beaconsfield	50
The Rt. Hon. W. E. Gladstone on his 79th Birthday	52
Mother's Boy	53
Our Cemetery	55
Shipwreck'd	57
An Appeal	58
Sunderland Calamity	60
In Memoriam—Lord Fredk. Cavendish ...	62

CONTENTS.

ii.

	PAGE.
Lily May	64
Homeless	71
A Satire	73
Song—Wandering Boy	77
Song—Wandering Boy's Return	78
A Christmas Eve's Vision	79
An Impromptu Farewell	84
Woman's Mission	85
In Memoriam—Mrs. Lang Bridge	88
Man's Inhumany	90
Bitter Memories, or, the Ballet Girl's Remorse	97
Dedicated to the Rev. Thos. Waugh	100
Dedicated to the Rev. R. Catterall	102
Honour to Christ	103
Spirit Love	106
Rich and Poor	110
In Memoriam—Wm. Bury, Esq.	114
Jealousy	115
A Contrast	117
She's only Gone to Sleep	121
In Memoriam—Alexr. Hargreaves	122
The Muse	124
In Memoriam—Mrs. Jno. Bury	126
The Pauper	128
In Memoriam—Edwin Waugh	131
Remember the Poor	133
In Memoriam—Mrs. Newell	136
In Memoriam—Albert Dobson	138
In Memoriam—Alice Higham	139
Hymn on the Death of Eli Higham, junior	141
A Voice from Beyond	143
In Memoriam—Miss Annie Williams	144
In Memoriam—Dr. Clayton	146

www.ingramcontent.com/pod-product-compliance
Lightning Source LLC
Chambersburg PA
CBHW022129160426
43197CB00009B/1209